MILLION DOLLAR MINDSET

7 Keys to Creating the Life You Want

TIANA VON JOHNSON

DISCLAIMER AND/OR LEGAL NOTICES

While all attempts have been made to verify information provided in this book and its ancillary materials, neither the author nor publisher assumes responsibility for errors, inaccuracies, or omissions and is not responsible for any monetary loss in any matter. If advice concerning legal, financial, accounting or related matters is needed, the services of a qualified professional should be sought. This book or is associated ancillary materials, including verbal and written training, is not intended for use as a source of legal, financial, or accounting advice. You should be aware of the various laws governing business transactions or other business practices in your state. The information contained in this book is strictly for educational purpose. Therefore, if you wish to apply ideas contained in this book, you are taking full responsibility for your actions. There is no guarantee or promise, expressed or implied, that you will earn any money using the strategies, concepts, techniques, exercises and ideas in the book.

STANDARD EARNINGS AND INCOME DISCLAIMER

With respect to the reliability, accuracy, timeliness, usefulness, adequacy, completeness, and/or suitability of information provided in this book, TVJ Worldwide, LLC. its partners' associates, affiliates, consultants, and/or presenters make no warranties, guarantees, representations, or claims of any kind. Participants' results will vary depending on many factors. All claims or representations as to income earning are not considered as average earnings. All products and services are for educational and informational purposes only. Check with your accountant, attorney, or professional advisor before acting on this or any information. By continuing with reading this book, you agree that TVJ Worldwide, LLC. is not responsible for the success or failure of your personal, business, or financial decisions relating to any information.

PRINTED IN THE UNITED STATES OF AMERICA | FIRST EDITION

Dedication

This book is dedicated to the people who are just like I was, when I was trying to figure life out. Those bursting with ambition, joyfully leaving yesterday behind, and passionately working towards a better future. I believe in you!

Acknowledgments

First, I want to thank God for blessing me with gifts and putting it in my spirit to write this book. I would also like to thank Jack Redmond for many long hours planning, reviewing content, reorganizing, writing, re-writing, and making decisions to bring this project to completion—I am so proud! I could not have done it without you. To Percy Miller aka Master P, thank you for blessing me by writing the foreword—your endorsement means a lot to me.

To my daily support team, I can't say thank you enough for your many hours of counsel, love and support. My king, my sweetheart, my love Thor, thank you for loving me, growing with me and doing this thing called life with me. My young kings, Taliem & Tristen Johnson, thank you for understanding that "Mommy had to work all these years." You are growing to be amazing men! My father King George Johnson, thank you for instilling your entrepreneurialism in me. My mother "Cookie," thank you for instilling your creative genius in me. My grandmother Mama, thank you for always telling me that I'm the cutest one in the family (wink)! My uncle Greg, thank you for being my mentor and therapist when I needed it most. My cousin Dr. Pebbles Riley (Pebblee Poo), thank you for the tears, laughter and rocking with me and investing in every project. My bestie D'or Reed-Jordan, do not ever stop being you, thank for always being there for me through the good, the bad and the ugly. Susan Bond, thank you for all of your support and taking all my many calls when I needed you most. Dr. Stacie NC Grant, thank you for years of prayer and support. My godbrother, Raiheen Bell, thank for doing anything possible to get the job done for over 20 years and sorry for firing and rehiring you 20 times! Dan Sorrell, you are a genius at what you do. Thank you for sharing your gifts with me for so many years. To all my brothers, the late Elijah Johnson, Jamal Johnson, J-Quan Johnson, Jakeal Johnson and Devin Johnson—I love you all so much. To everyone I call my friend, my family and extended family, my soon-to-be-in laws and stepchildren, thank you! To all my clients, followers and fans, a super big thank you!

TABLE OF KEYS

MILLION DOLLAR MINDSET

7 Keys to Creating the Life You Want

TIANA VON JOHNSON

FORWARD BY PERCY MILLER aka MASTER P

5x Grammy Award Winning Mogul, Entrepreneur, Rapper, Actor,
Investor, Author, Filmmaker, Record Producer & Philanthropist

Almost everyone I meet wants to make more money, but few have the right mindset or game plan to reach this goal. In the *Million Dollar Mindset*, Tiana Von Johnson gives you the roadmap by sharing her keys to creating the life you want. I would highly recommend this book to anyone who desires significant life change because these keys are powerful and necessary. Many of these keys I learned through trial and error, with no mentorship or guidance. I learned for myself, then seen in countless others, that if you can change the way you think, you can change the way you live.

Early on, I realized that how I think would set the direction for my life. I came a long way from selling CDs from my trunk to producing and selling movies, launching sneaker lines, food products, and continuing decades of music production and sales. Yes, I have made and will continue to make millions, but more importantly, I want to leave a legacy for my family and teach the next generation.

I came from poverty and decided to educate myself to do more. I made it and want to give people a blueprint for success. So much pain has come from a lack of education. I now teach entrepreneurs how they can succeed through the "Master P Masterclass," which is a live teaching series in various cities— MasterPMasterClass.com. Tiana has become one of my business partners on this initiative because of her discipline, insatiable desire to help people, and steadfast commitment to hard work. This has positioned her to live well and earned her the right to teach others.

Tiana has smashed glass ceilings, torn down walls and blazed new trails to become a millionaire. She has successfully overcome all of the societal roadblocks to build multiple businesses and launch major projects. She takes responsibility for mistakes, learns through failing, honed her leadership skills, and still helps others attain wealth. In meeting and working with her, I have seen her passion and results. She reminds me of myself!

The journey to becoming a millionaire starts in your mind and this book will help you develop the MILLION DOLLAR MINDSET and create the life you want—and deserve!

PERCY MILLER
MASTER P

INTRODUCTION

"Just get started and get it done, there will never be a perfect time."

—*Tiana Von Johnson*

I'm not here to be average or live a normal life. You get one life to live, and I decided long ago that I would live a great life. I chose to kick down doors, break glass ceilings, and where society's paths and systems said "No," I took a different path. I refuse man-made limitations, and I am determined to live out my purpose- and with style!

I Am a Problem!

I am a problem to any stagnant mindset, system, or individual that seeks to keep people living less than who God created them to be. I am a problem to the status quo that neverendingly tries to suck people into average and keep them there. I hate to see people live beneath their potential. I exist to help people progress into being more than their current situation—often more than what their family could ever imagine them to be. People committed to mediocrity will never like me!

I Am a Fighter

I have had to fight my whole life. As a child, I fought against a system designed to produce mediocre people who live safe lives, punch a clock from 9-to-5 and hope that someday they will be able to survive on Social Security and their pension. I was an average student who grew up going back and forth between parents. I stood in line with my mom for public assistance and watched her struggle as she fought through the harsh realities of life. No silver spoon, no inheritance, no mentor, no great connections, just a dream and a whole lot of hard work.

I fought the fears of leaving my safe job, making over 6 figures as a single mom. When I launched my first business, a real estate brokerage in New York City, I had to fight my previous broker spreading lies about me, stealing my domain name, TianaVonJohnson.com, and trying to blackball me. I fought the pain of friends and family cutting me off. I fought fears, loneliness, and many other things that no one knows about. No one handed me anything, I had to fight every day on many levels.

I Am Going

As a child, when people asked me what I was going to be, I would tell them that I was going to be a businesswoman. When everyone else was trying to figure out how to survive, I was trying to figure out how I was going to become a millionaire. I was determined to make this journey—period! I was determined that I was going to make it and make it big.

I Take Risks

All my life, there was something in me to take risks and not settle for what life handed me. You will never succeed at great things by playing it safe. I'm not saying to be foolish, but I think that playing it safe your whole life is long-term foolishness! We need to be smart, learn about all aspects of our endeavors, but at some point, you can't get to your destiny and purpose without risk. You can settle for less, but that is what you will get—less.

No risk means at best, you will live an average life. Average is not evil, but it is average, and honestly, in most cases, average does not end up good. Living an average life is like eating unseasoned food. It's safe, it will sustain you, but it's hard to enjoy!

I Am a Lifelong Learner

It was not until I got older that I realized that two of my greatest teachers were my parents. I thank God for both of them and what they taught me. As I traveled back and forth between their homes growing up, I was able to learn different things. I developed a skill for negotiation and a love for entrepreneurship, helping my father sell records on the streets of Harlem. I honed my creative genius by watching my mother do hair, sew, cook, make dolls, and design flowers. This helped me, and I combined the entrepreneurial and creative skills of both of my parents, and I developed a knack for making money!

I Was a Young Money Maker!

When I was in elementary school, we had to sell chocolate bars for $1 for our school fundraiser—I sold each bar for $2 and kept $1 for myself! Then there were the free circulars that companies would leave on peoples doors and cars. I would collect them and sell them for a quarter. I think people knew they were free and they either thought I was cute or felt bad for me but either way, they would give me a quarter. I would also knock on people's doors and offer to clean their yard for $5. I would throw around their garbage a bit beforehand to make it look messy before I offered to clean it. Looking back, I'm not proud of that (or taking and reselling the circulars) but, let's just say that it was my way to get them to understand that they really needed my services—wink!

My mother would also make different kinds of crafts and I would take out a towel and lay it out in front of my grandmother's house where we lived. I would sell her pieces to people walking by for extra money. I also negotiated a deal with the local Carvel ice cream shop around the corner from my house to call me every time they had "mistakums." This was the name I created for cakes that had misspellings or ice cream that was made, and the customer changed their mind. Instead of throwing them away, the salesperson would wrap them and call me to come get them. I would rush the ice creams back to the house and sell them to my neighbors for half the price! The rush of creating businesses and making money for myself made me happy.

I Don't Like the Traditional Education and Business Route

I graduated high school, then earned a Bachelor's degree at 20 and had a Master's degree by 21. I applied for a doctorate but got rejected because they told me that I was too young. The reality was that I did this because society told me this was the way to success and stability. In my thinking, if I was going to take this path, I was going to do it big. I didn't feel it would get me to where I wanted, but I did it anyway.

I worked in human resources for 8 years. Even though I hated my job, I was good at it. I started out at 40K per year as an HR manager and worked my way up with multiple promotions both within and by switching companies until I was making over 6 figures by 26-years-old. I was "living the dream" and envied by many, but deep down, I couldn't stand working for someone else every day and not living my passion and dreams.

I Do What I Love

Being unfulfilled in my job, I did what I loved on weekends. I produced all kinds of events, such as fashion shows, dance competitions, and real estate and business seminars. My creative juices flowed. I love the planning, building my team and then executing it. The more I enjoyed my weekends, the more I resented Mondays.

I found myself sitting at work but thinking about my business and worked extra hard to finish up the tasks of my job so that I could focus on what I loved. I realized I was doing a disservice to both myself and my employer. I realized that I needed to go; it was too much! I just didn't like being there; the redundancy was stifling. I remember one of my employees was making $28,000 after working for

28 years at the job! I couldn't imagine working so long for so little, and this was just one of many scenarios.

I Quit My Job

In 2009, I was done. I quit my regular job and knew it was time to pursue my dreams. Around this time, we were going through a tough time in our economy, and while people were trying to find jobs, I was quitting mine. I figured it was now or never, and my dreams could no longer wait.

So, I put in a 6-week resignation letter, but this is when fear really began to set in, and I began to get nervous. I was so afraid that I started looking for a new job. I could have stayed at my old job, but because I told everyone that I was going to be an entrepreneur, my ego wouldn't let me stay. I was scared because I didn't have a plan, so I quit and then got a new job.

My last day was Friday and I started the new job on Monday—and took a 20K pay cut to save face. By lunchtime I was miserable! Being a single mom made it even tougher. I had to get my kids to daycare by 8 a.m. and then get to work by 9 a.m. I found myself skipping from the train to my workplace to get there faster than I could walk. One day I got to work at 9:05 a.m., and my boss was looking at me and staring at his watch. I knew this was not for me.

One day I went down to Wall Street, and I remember telling myself that I would make my first million dollars here but had no idea how. I went on an interview with a real estate agency and got hired. I didn't have the startup money, so I borrowed $350 from a friend to get my real estate license.

I closed my first deal! I made $4500 in my first 45 minutes and I felt "I can do this." Our broker said anyone that can make 20 deals in a month would get a

$5000 bonus, and I got it. I made a total of $80K, which I split with my broker since I was on a 50/50 commission. It felt good to make $40K, but my thinking hadn't changed yet, and I used it to pay bills and go shopping. About a month later, I realized that I needed to brand myself and go harder than ever before.

When others would make 2-3 real estate ads per day, I would create 50-60 and began to brand myself as the "Celebrity Real Estate Agent," even though I had no celebrity clients. When I started marketing myself this way, I began to get calls from celebrities who were looking to buy or rent in New York City. My strategy worked!

The money was great, but I soon realized that 50% of the money I earned was going to the brokerage I was working for, and I began to think about what it would look like if I was able to receive 100% of the commissions. I began to plan the launch of my own real estate company, Goldstar Properties, and I told my current broker. Days later, they offered me $250,000 to stay and become a partner. It was a tough decision, but I decided to turn it down. If I took the deal, they would practically own me. It felt like blood money. It felt like I was going against everything that I fought so hard for by leaving my 9-to-5 job. Imagine turning down a quarter of a million dollars! Taking the money would have been conventional wisdom, desperate and thirsty, but would have cost me millions and my pride in the long run!

Real Estate Was My Door and Training Ground

I have been blessed in the world of real estate. Because I approached it with the right mindset, I have been able to develop innovative initiatives that are helping people, especially minorities, all over America. In a world of many broke and frustrated real estate agents, I chose a different mindset that caused me to excel in a down market, and now I get to help others do the same. I have seen the helplessness that comes along with the mindset that we are all told to exercise. It does not work. That kind of mindset these days is bad—like throwing a live zebra into a cage of hungry lions.

I generated my first million dollars at age 27—my first year in business. I have achieved success, and believe me, it is lonely at the top. Some people hate it when you succeed because it makes them feel bad about their own lives. But these conditioned people have no idea how hard you had to work. The choice is simple. Do I stay the same or live differently?

According to Richard LeFrak, a billionaire real estate investor, he said he could not achieve success without his family. That was a big aha moment for me because I realized that in my culture, we do not put our money together and invest it with our families. We save, and save, and HOPE for better days. But the reality is that we are saving pennies and dollars. We were not taught to pool money together to create real generational wealth. The only pooling of funds we ever really did with our families, friends and coworkers, was an informal savings clubs, also known as a "susu." This approach simply can't get us to where we want to go long-term.

I had a choice for a little over five years. I could either continue to comfortably make millions on my own or try to bring as many people with me as I could. This was not an easy decision. When it comes to some of "our people," everything is a scam, and they will not read or take the time to learn anything new about other successful business ventures. It was a hefty challenge! But I did it anyway.

I started a coaching and mastermind club to join and collaborate with business-minded entrepreneurs, in any industry, across the country. The club allows business owners to get coached by me and to network and create joint ventures to make more money together.

There are millions to be had if we work on them both individually and together. But more important than knowledge is the mindset! You can give two people an opportunity and information, and one will seize it and make millions while the other will just keep doing the same things, complain, and get the same results.

Today, I have several businesses while training hundreds of entrepreneurs simultaneously. I don't worry about what I don't know, I attack and destroy any lack of knowledge that keeps me from success. My constant passion for learning has allowed me to become the only African-American real estate broker on Wall Street today and one of only a few in the board game industry. Every business I create is by choice, and my decision to do something, figure it out, and learn along the way. Constant learning and doing means constant progress.

I Am a Survivor

I survived growing up in the Bronx, where many others ended up in bad situations. I survived as a single parent when my son's father, was shot and killed. I survived a poor educational system to become a lifelong learner and multimillionaire. I survived verbal abuse. I survived all the traditional norms of life. I survived the temptation of quick money. I always had that entrepreneurial spirit and wanted to make money and fast—I remember thinking, "Maybe I should be a stripper" or "Maybe I should sell drugs." These were the options. I survived that statistic and did not go down that road. But I did become another statistic—a single mother. I had a second child by 25-years-old and although I love my sons, it felt terrible being a "baby mama," twice. However, even with that perception, I pushed through.

I am a survivor of business and entrepreneurial trials, failures, and sabotages. Some of these include personal bankruptcy, foreclosure, and almost a half a million dollars of IRS debt until this day. A lot of this came from trial and error and learning. I am digging myself out of holes like this resulting from my trial and error and not having mentors to come in and teach me how to work with money.

I had my first house at 26 and lost it by 27. This became one of the driving forces for my entrepreneurialism because my 9-to-5 job could not sustain my mortgage. This was so embarrassing because it was my dream house. I was so happy, and then I lost it. I was so ashamed that I told people I moved, because how can you tell people that you lost your house to foreclosure?

The bottom line is that I have been there. I've been backstabbed and lied about by people I thought were my friends and who I made a lot of money, for and with! This too drove me to become my own boss! In the end, I survived it all. It made me stronger, smarter, and wiser.

I Am a Conqueror

A conqueror is someone that faces life's fights and wins. I have a great mind and can overcome great obstacles and trials. I am not perfect, and I don't know everything, but I know how to keep going, keep learning, and keep winning. Conquerors don't live average lives hoping things will be okay. They see new opportunities, and they go after them. People were taught not to chase money and dreams, but I beg to differ. You have to run this race like it's a marathon!

I Am Just Like You

I laugh. I cry. I bleed. I get scared, lonely, and even overwhelmed at times. People have hurt me. I have been cheated on. Friends, family, and clients have stabbed me in the back so many times. What gets me through this, is that I have learned to trust God to help me in tough times, and I have learned to trust myself, my gifts, and my instincts. I decided not to harbor my hurt. Instead, I chose to see the people who have hurt me as people who really need this book!

My faith and experience have taught me that I am in a relationship with God. He is my Creator and designed me with talents, intellect, and intuition. He also leads and strengthens me along the way. I have learned to trust Him when I don't understand things, lean on Him for strength, and to pray and ask for guidance. But once received, I must act, and work to get it done. He will lead me in the right direction, but I have to go. He has given me tremendous talents and gifts, but I must put them to work. In business terms, He is my CEO, who provides the vision, direction, and empowerment, but it is up to me to create and execute the plan.

I Am Me

Take it or leave, I am, who I am. I believe that now is my time, and I will take hold of all that God has for me. I am not stuck. I am not a victim, and I refuse limits. My goal in life is to be the best me, and I hope to help you be the best you!

The Miracle of Mindset Change

It took me years and a lot of hard-won experience, and struggle to realize that I was born into what I believe was a type of prison. Growing up in the Bronx, New York, I absorbed the mindset of the people around me, as we all do. I did not realize that if I accepted this mindset, it would determine my entire life path.

Because of the way I thought about myself and the world, I constructed a mental cage that locked me down into a lifestyle that I did not want for myself. Looking back, it was my rebellion against this lifestyle that caused me to break the chains and free myself.

Of course, there is a massive disconnect between wanting to escape your circumstances and being able to do it. The reality is that most people are unable to change the circumstances they have created for themselves or life and societal norms forced them into. We are told a lot of things growing up that make us accept that things "just are" the way they are. Too few people ever realize that they are in control of their own lives.

This is why I am writing this book. It is for you, your daughters, sons, sisters, brothers, aunts, uncles, your mother, your father—the people in your life who want to break away from the "poverty" or "status quo" mindset and excel in life. There is abundance out there. You just have to look inside yourself.

Imagine that! The answer to your dysfunctional lifestyle is not on the outside; it is on the inside! Your mind and how it has been programmed dictates what you can and cannot achieve. That is fact. Struggle is a dysfunction, and it causes a lot of pain, heartache, and emotional trauma. Existing in a small, closed-off world was never God's plan for us.

In this book, I will teach you how to reject your current mental programming and replace it with a mindset that leads to success, happiness, and fulfillment. It is my chance to give back—for all the blessings that the Lord has given me in my life. If you let me, I will help you change your mindset and your life.

Life from Two Perspectives

Have you ever wondered why some people rise above their circumstances and succeed while others are forced to live below the "surface" of life—like we are all underwater, waiting for another opportunity to take a breath? We all have personal struggles due to bad decisions. If you cannot control your decisions, you cannot control your life.

The Bronx, New York, was a rough place to grow up. All around me there were signs and experiences that indicated this would be my "forever," and it always scared me. I think it scares everyone. The fear of having nothing, BEING nothing—it is a terrifying thing to grow up with.

My friend Danielle and I both decided that we wanted more out of life before life had even happened to us yet. We were just young girls attending C.I.S. 229 in the South Bronx. We were best friends with big hopes and dreams. We were not into cutting school, sneaking out at lunchtime, or smoking in the school hallways like other kids. All we wanted to do was play "businesswomen" and dream big. Sure, we wanted to look good and have money, that was the ultimate back then, but our families were struggling.

After a few years, Danielle lost her mother and had to move out of state. I was left alone and heartbroken, but I put my plan of success into action. Danielle chose to find her way by following the "traditional" mindset. You know the one because you were probably told the same thing when you were growing up. Stay in school, study hard, get a job, start a family. Everything will be okay. But things were never okay. People wait for that "okay" their entire lives where I am from.

I always suspected that "okay" was a false promise. Maybe it was good advice 30 or 40 years ago, but today it does not count for anything. You cannot rely on "conventional wisdom" passed down by your parents when they had many of their own problems like poverty, struggle, and economic hardship.

Conventional wisdom is actually becoming less effective as our economy and society changes. People cannot save, pensions are rare or insufficient, Social Security is not guaranteed, and the cost of living is rising at rates greater than retirement incomes and additional part-time jobs can afford, so many retired people cannot even cover basic living expenses. Many have put their hope in a system that literally CANNOT give them what they either want or need!

Danielle chose to live through her early adult years, trying to become successful by doing the "traditional" thing. I did something different. Due to my circumstances, I needed a big change, something that would guarantee my prosperity. It was God's plan that I was made to live through the experiences that forced me to re-evaluate my choices and my mindset—and I have never looked back.

The Path Forward

I was broken but graduated with my Master of Business Administration at 21-years-old, working a 9-to-5 job and feeling a major void in my life. Danielle, on the other hand, was happy; she knuckled down and worked hard in her job. She was getting by and flowing through life the way society told her, and I was broken. I knew that I had to do something. I could not just live a "normal life" like everyone else around me. I was tired, and I was not going to allow my son to grow up as I did. I had to get out of there; I had to do something—something different than what Danielle and every other person I knew was doing.

Aiming High Means Reaching Higher

If you are the kind of person who hopes every day for an increase at work, a drop in the gas price, a tax return, or a few days off your long, hard job, you are taking part in a system that is founded on hopelessness. Even if these things go your way, they will only be a few dollars in your pocket and will probably be erased by other increases in rent, food prices, property taxes, or whatever. How will you make tens or hundreds of thousands of dollars more each year? So many people work for years to get a dollar an hour raise or a 1-3% salary increase but when you do the math, after taxes, you will literally make $25-$30 extra per week.

You cannot live life like that. The moment I recognized the problem, it only took me a few years to bounce back and start my career as a trailblazer in business. I instantly fell in love with entrepreneurship, running my own company, the process, and making deals happen to provide for my two sons. Never forget the generational impact that your mindset has. How you think directs how you live, which affects the entire trajectory of your children and the generations that follow. My father's street entrepreneurial instincts sowed the seeds for me to be a millionaire, and my children's normal is entirely different from my normal growing up.

I went from living paycheck-to-paycheck, a broken single parent in the Bronx who was trapped in relationships with zebra-like mindsets, to being the only African-American, multi-million dollar real estate brokerage owner on Wall Street, self-made millionaire mogul, speaker, author, filmmaker, game inventor, magazine publisher, business coach, beauty brand owner, event producer, and so much more!

I literally had no one helping me. No role models, mentors or people working on my behalf. If anything, I had the deck stacked against me but still won the game, and I keep on winning. Excuse me for saying so, but if I can do it, so can you. You can do it because God has put gifts in you and wired you for success. You also have the power of choice, decisions, and the ability to plan success and navigate the obstacles of life. Always remember that YOUR decisions decide your wealth. You are not a product of your circumstances; you are a product of your decisions.

Sometimes life pushes you so far down that your only choice is to reach as high as you can to get the heck out of there. I have been reaching high ever since. Real estate was not my true passion, but it gave me everything I needed and continues to provide me with amazing opportunities. I used real estate as a vehicle to finance my true passions and dreams.

Rejecting the Trapped Mindset

When I look back at my early mistakes, it really helped me wake up. I was in a dire situation. I needed to make a potentially life-changing decision about who I wanted to be in the world. I had no idea what to do, where to go, or how to get there. I only knew that what I had been doing—and what the people around me had been doing (sorry Danielle!)—was not the path I wanted to go down. I did not want to have a small, trapped mind anymore. My mind was desperate for growth, learning, and understanding.

I knew that there must be something "else" that successful people understood that I just had not come across yet. I guess the moment I started asking the right questions was when I started finding the right answers.

- Why do I allow myself to struggle from day-to-day?
- What could I do to create financial stability for myself and my family?
- What do I have to learn to become a successful mind?
- Who do I have to invest in—a coach, mentor, educator?
- What conferences do I have to attend to learn more than I know?
- What books do I have to read that will teach me how to reach success?

I realized that there are two types of mindsets in the world. The first type of mindset is the "trapped or fixed" mindset. These are people that "accept" their circumstances. They follow the "system" or prescribed "method" of life. These minds accept that they can only hope to achieve what is in their current "ability" or "power" to achieve.

The other type of mindset is the "growth or free" mindset. This mind follows their own path. They reject that they can only achieve based on what they "know," and they seek to learn, evolve, and develop all the time.

I hate to say this, but many people are living with a trapped mindset. You suffer from a lack of money, serious debt, and untold stress because you cannot find a way out of your current circumstances. You react to life instead of creating one that you want to live in.

I know because I have experienced both types of mindsets. In many ways, you feel like the "system" could not have possibly failed you like that, but it has. Getting a job and working hard will not make you rich or successful. Only one thing can, and that is YOU!

I am blown away by the number of people that are being forced to live off "low-income retirement" because they never reached financial success. There are generations of people every year that are retiring with the harsh reality that their struggles will only get worse. Think about that!

If you do not believe that being financially stable is incredibly important, then you have not thought about it long enough. Money is not just money, it is life. God wants you to prosper and succeed, yet you willingly hand over your fate to a system that has already failed you.

You need to realize that inside your mind is power far beyond anything that you have imagined up until now. Reaching your personal potential is one of the many goals that help you attain spiritual fulfillment, emotional health, and mental happiness in life. Everyone is born with a mind perfectly geared to meet their own needs. But the choice also exists, as you know! You have to choose to unlock that potential!

I found out that I was able to achieve more than I had ever dreamed possible simply by having faith, being proactive, getting things done, and placing myself where I knew I needed to be. When my mindset changed, my life changed. It is time to free yourself from that trapped mindset!

Embracing Your Personal Potential

I believe that God has blessed each and every one of us with the personal potential to be exactly who we want to be. Life is just a process of finding out who or what that is. There is a formula that results in success, but it does not exist in the external world.

It starts, plays, and finishes in your mind. What you believe right now makes up who you are. It is belief that dictates what we think and thought that dictates how we behave. If you want your behavior to change, then you need to start with your mind.

Think of it this way—there is a very good reason why you go to work every day. You understand that you need a paycheck and that working will get you one. You get up in the morning, drag yourself to work, and sit there all day for the sole purpose of earning money.

This entire process is built on the assumed belief that IF YOU WORK HARD, a day will come when you have enough money. There is a silent promise of a better future that never comes. Consider this—things are not improving. What if I proved to you that working in your job for the rest of your life will NOT result in financial success? But I think you already know that. Let's move to Key # 1!

Key #1

Deserving Wealth

"Do the one thing you think you cannot do. Fail at it. Try again. Do better the second time. The only people who never tumble are those who never mount the high wire. This is your moment. Own it."

—*OPRAH WINFREY*

If you want to master your mind, then you must begin with the most fundamental question—do you deserve to be wealthy? I am not talking about morality or anything like that—just you, as you are now. Do you deserve wealth?

For those in poverty, your beliefs can and ARE preventing you from transcending poverty. You currently believe that you should be poor, and so you are. In today's day and age, it's not only the poor who are poor! Another growing group is stuck in "mediocrity" and are functionally poor. Many middle-class people who make 6 figures literally have a small or even negative net worth. People who would traditionally be well off now carry excessive mortgages, have 2 car payments, and live paycheck-to-paycheck while carrying growing and never-ending credit card and student loan debt. Many people in the "middle class" are literally one or two paychecks away from being homeless. These people dreamed of making lots of money and now go through life financially and emotionally empty. These people are stuck in the limitations of their mindset. Let me explain.

Your Complicated Relationship with Money

Most of the middle class, or poorer classes, hate money—they hate it! Because of the way they were brought up, they learned to believe that money was always a scarce thing and that it should be treated like it was sacred, special, or ultimately meaningful.

I had a very complicated relationship with money. I knew I needed more of it, and I hated that. Indirectly, I guess I hated money. It never seemed to go anywhere or DO anything for me. I spent a lot of time working and very little time enjoying the money I earned from my incredibly hard work. Something was wrong.

Then you get the flip side of that—loving money. Danielle loved earning her paycheck. It was validation that she had worked hard. But because she loved her money so much, she would deprive herself of a better quality of life to hang onto what was essentially paper. Did it make her any richer? Not at all.

So, love it or hate it, we all have funny ideas about money. Perched at the core of all of these complicated feelings is a belief system about money. Your belief system is unconsciously controlling the way you respond to money in your life. It is the reason why you have so much debt and so little cash flow. In essence, your mindset determines whether or not you "deserve wealth."

Many believe money is evil! Believe me, it is not. In the hands of a good person, money is the single most powerful natural tool that can drive positive social change in the world. Money pays the bills. True, but what about life after your bills? If you are only working to cover your expenses, you are not earning for any kind of life.

Being financially secure is an important life goal. Without money, you will not ever be able to experience the things that you were meant to experience on this earth. Stop seeing money as the enemy. It is no enemy of mine. Instead, give your shame, guilt, and bad feelings about money to God to begin the healing process. Money is a good thing.

Self-Investment Comes First

When I was just realizing that I did not want to earn a pittance for the rest of my life, at the same time, I chatted with Danielle about her money. During the conversation, I noticed that Danielle had no plans whatsoever to do anything other than save the money she earned. She had no plans to increase her job's current income, create additional income streams, or own anything that would put her in a better financial situation. In essence, she was firmly committed to walk and run on a never-ending treadmill, always working but never getting anywhere new or better. That meant in 20 years of saving that Danielle would still be poor—with a tiny little nest egg. This was not good enough for me. I knew I had to do something, but I was not taught how.

I realized later in life that this was not my fault, and it is not your fault. Many of us were only afforded a public-school education, and money education and entrepreneurship were not the focus. The basic focus of public education was to train people to be productive workers and citizens. If you do not know about money, you become a victim of the money system. That is why one of the best things that you can do to change your mindset about money is to get to know it. Invest in your own knowledge about money first so that everything else can click into place.

- Are your bills out of control?
- Do you understand that money should be invested in something for growth?
- Did you know that money can generate money?

Self-investment is about making yourself aware of the money-world around you. They will not teach you about money at school. They do not teach you about money when you start your first job. It is absolutely your responsibility to learn how money works.

People think that just because it is not part of our education system that it is not important. But what could be more important than money to anyone and everyone that wants to be successful? There is a HUGE gap in knowledge that you need to fill.

That is why I began to invest in my money education. I started at a young age when I began selling records with my father on the streets of Harlem, New York. This grew into a keen interest in earning—and HOW to earn—which helped set me on this path. Watching my father "hustle" records and how he negotiated with buyers made my antennas go up. I realized then that money was my friend, but I had to work hard on my own to get it and was willing to do it. I was learning.

I also learned that there was a "street smart" money mindset and a "business smart" money mindset. Many of the entrepreneurs I work with and train do not have high-level degrees, but they use their wit, street-savvy, and intelligence combined with practical knowledge gained to excel in building wealth.

Commit right now to invest in your money knowledge. You cannot rely on anyone else to figure out how money works. The only way you are going to get a handle on it is to learn for yourself. It is one of the greatest life skills you can build on. Of course, you can (and should) attend seminars, but make sure the educators really understand wealth and have achieved wealth on their own.

Adopting a 3D Perspective on Wealth

I always hear people saying, "I wish I was rich," and "If I only had X, I could do Y"—but this way of thinking is not helpful, and honestly, it still passes the buck. You have to adopt a 3D perspective on wealth if you want to learn how to be wealthy.

Being "wealthy" is not a state of having money. It is a process of learning how to create, invest, and manage money. It requires learning, and it certainly requires time. What you do not realize about money is that it is there for the taking. You have the talent and power to reach out and attract whatever amount you want. People say, "money does not grow on trees," but I say YES IT DOES!

27

You just have to be willing to climb up the tree and get it.

Money, like anything else, requires rules. Most people do not apply the right rules, so they do not get the right results. Imagine for a moment that someone gave you $100, and you had to go into the world and create more money from this amount. What would you do? Sure, you can buy something worth that amount and sell it for profit. But then you have to do that again and again until you have the amount that you want. Simple, yet you will have needs along the way and will probably use some of that money until none is left.

Alongside money, there is the quality of life. This is a HUGE consideration that people forget about. You have to understand money and how to make money while still living with the quality of life that you want. How do you make this happen? Pay attention to the details. Money leaves a paper trail, so get into the habit of examining, analyzing, and working with that trail. Make time for money. You make time for your kids, your family, your work, your friends, and even people you do not like. But you spend NO time with your money. Why?

The average person claims to not have enough money, but if you ask them a few questions, most people will eventually blurt out something like, "I don't know where it all goes," which is both a true and telling statement. These people work incredibly hard, are very frustrated because they don't have enough, and literally cannot tell you what happened to their most important commodity.

Make it a priority. Money must be at the top of your priority list. Food comes first, yes—but money buys food. That makes it more important. This is your life! My point is that "wealth" is not something that just happens. Ask the many, many people that have won the lottery, and it has ruined their lives. They lose everything and end up in enormous debt for the rest of their days, all because they believed that "wealth" was a state of being and not something that you have to EARN.

Wealth is earned, managed, and tracked by the upper classes. That is why I want you to learn the 3 Ds of money—Discover, Discuss, and Deploy!

- **Discover.** How do you earn money? Where does it go? What does it do? Where are you losing money? How can you make more of it?

- **Discuss.** Verify what you have learned by discussing it. Come up with a game plan, create a wealth strategy, and start putting your money to work.

- **Deploy.** Work through the stages of your plan. Learn from your mistakes and find out what you are good at. Make money from money and build your wealth.

The Integral Role of Learning in Wealth

If someone received an inheritance or made a sizable amount of money, they would usually talk to a financial advisor who would invest their money for them. Here is the problem that I have with that. Often the financial advisor has no money themselves, yet they sell financial advice.

I am only going to say this once and for all—only trust yourself with your money. You need to know where it is, what it is doing, and how it is making those things happen. Attempt to understand what you can or cannot do with it so that YOU can make the right decisions. The reason why the poor and middle classes do not have much money is specifically because many of them give it to other people. This means they can never learn from their own mistakes, improve their strategies, or work in their own best interests.

Another reason we lack knowledge and understanding is that many of us are following in our parents' footsteps. They either lacked the knowledge or pathways to build and create wealth, so they could not teach us what they did not know.

This has driven me to be a trainer and coach to others, but first, I had to learn. Next, I committed to teaching my sons and then teaching anyone and everyone who wants to learn to build wealth. If we want to see our family, friends, and community uplifted into greater wealth, we must help others gain this knowledge, wisdom, and courage to live differently. However, it begins with us learning for ourselves.

If you do not have a process of trial and error—or failure and success—how are you ever going to expect to have the knowledge to manage millions? It just does not happen in the real world. I know, because I have lost my share of money along my journey. It is part of the process.

I did not have people to teach me how to manage and grow money. I found myself in debt and owing loads to student loans and the IRS while running my business. After I started to have a better relationship with and understanding of money—and after a lot of trial and error—I learned how to manage money successfully. That means I had not only attained money—I had learned how to manage, invest, and secure my wealth to maintain my chosen quality of life.

One of the key lessons I have learned is to take responsibility or own what I do. Don't wait for anyone else or expect people to help you--for free! Educate yourself, take risks, hire a coach but don't blame or wait for others. Be proactive, constantly grow, and keep moving forward. Whatever you do, own it!

You Can Only Be Rich When You Deserve the Money

The lesson here—be the kind of person that DESERVES wealth. Ignorance is nothing to be proud of, and while our culture and society tell us that it is okay to ignore the science of money, that does not mean they are right. Society is wrong!

Society tells you that you should not make ANY mistakes and that you must be nice and share with everyone. You can like money, but it is essentially a dirty, immoral thing; that only people who have worked extremely hard on their jobs and careers DESERVE.

This is all wrong! Wrong, wrong, wrong! To be truly deserving of money, you need to make LOTS of mistakes to gain experience with money management. You have to learn to say no to people and to put your financial interests first. Money is not a dirty thing; it can be the most incredible gift from God.

And finally, money only comes to those who deserve it by understanding how to work with money. Not in their jobs or careers—with money. You deserve to create and enjoy all the money that you want in your lifetime. Learn to love working with money and EARN your way to wealth. When you work with money, a funny thing happens. More money! It is the basis for the universal law of attraction.

The harder Danielle worked on her job, the harder I worked on understanding money and how I could make more. Essentially, she spent her time toiling on that treadmill, while I spent my time learning and growing. Financially speaking, I zoomed past Danielle very quickly in terms of earnings. Then I eventually completely surpassed her.

In the end, Danielle wanted to know what she had done wrong. I told her that she had done nothing wrong in a moral sense—but her mindset was simply guiding her in the wrong direction. Instead of "following the herd," she needed to reprogram herself for success.

However, I do not blame Danielle! If you grew up the way we did—with no one teaching you about money—you are not going to understand much about how success happens! The only people that do are the ones that actively choose to go and find out. It is really that simple—perhaps the easiest thing in the world. Or is it?

There is no way I could conclude this topic without discussing the power of tithing and giving. Tithing is very important to building wealth and allowing your money to multiply. One of my foundational principles in building wealth is first putting my faith in God, not in money, and committing to being generous with my wealth. Tithing is a principle taught throughout the Bible where you give the first 10% of your income to the house of God, and His Work. It establishes God as our source, not a person, or business. This is one way that sets God as the priority in your life.

Tithing and giving overall also demonstrates confidence in your ability to continue to earn more money over time through knowledge, wisdom, and hard work. I consistently give to my Church, charities and other organizations who help entrepreneurs. Giving back is critical for your success. If you do not give, money will not come back you.

Thinking in Units

How do I think with a million-dollar mindset? Everything I do or business I go into, I go into it with the thought of "How can I make a million dollars?" I ask myself, how many units I need to sell to make $1 million. If I create a $1000 product or service, I know I need 1000 "yes's" to reach $1 million. This doesn't mean that I will reach $1 million with every product or service, but I go into every product or service with this type of thinking.

This mindset is much different than the way the average person goes into business. Most people go and get a bunch of business cards, set up a website, and then think, "Let me go promote my business and make some money." Most people don't sit down and think about creating a million-dollar plan because they don't even think that generating a million dollars is possible in one lifetime.

I teach people to think about a million-dollar plan for everything that you touch. But to start, YES, you must have money. I call the processing of getting baseline financial resources, "stacking money."

Stacking Money

When I travel, a lot of people tell me that I have money, which is why I can build my business. Then they say, they can't build their business because they don't have money to start. To people that have no money, live paycheck-to-paycheck, or money is super tight, here is some simple advice.

First of all, you have to look at where your money is going. Everybody has money, but if you are spending your money on things that won't grow you, you're not going to grow your money.

Here are three simple things you can do to use your money wisely and in a way that will allow you to start or grow your business ventures:

1. Look at where you are spending your money.
2. Eliminate expenses that are not going to grow you.
3. Get "chunks of money."

Getting Chunks of Money

Getting "chunks of money" means you have to get something going that will bring you larger sums of money at one time. A 9-to-5 job or a part-time job is not going to do that—especially if it has to go right back out to pay bills. If you have a part time job making $15 an hour for 20 hours, after you subtract taxes, travel expenses, etc. you are not going to have any money left to build a business.

I tell people to get a part-time job that will get you full-time income like real estate because if you do one deal, you can make $4 to $5k. Produce an event where you can gather a lot of people and sell things. Sell a service that only requires your "brain", so you do not have to invest in inventory. Services can be coaching, personal training, teaching, etc. What can you do to make money like this that you can inject into your business? Another important factor when it comes to getting money chunks is how you present yourself. How you present yourself can also attract money.

Attracting Money

You have to master the art of attracting money. Money can come to you, but how does money see you? Do you look good? Are you set up to receive it? Do you have a plan? Do you know what you will do when the money comes? Why would the money come to you if you are going to blow it?

The average thinker doesn't even have a plan or know what you will do with the money you receive. You always have to think, what am I doing to attract money to me? You have to look in the mirror and ask yourself, "Do I look like money?" "What's the perception when people see me?"

You also have to go where the money is. What types of events do you find yourself in? Are you at events where there are other people with money in the room? Do you talk to other people with money? Ask yourself these questions and start making changes right now to start attracting money.

We still have a long way to go before your mindset has been changed, and you understand all the keys. You still have dozens of questions and might be afraid. I know how that feels. Rest assured that by the end of this book, you will understand what needs to be done. Let's get to Key #2.

Key # 2

Think Like a Leader

"Insanity is doing the same thing over and over and expecting a different result."

—*Albert Einstein*

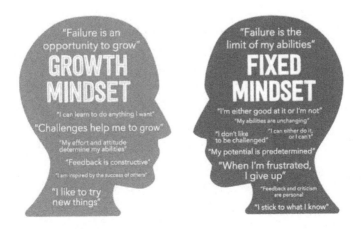

Growth vs. Fixed Mindsets

One of the greatest battles I had to win to transition from mediocrity to a million-dollar mindset was the battle in my mind. I had been conditioned by both stagnant and harsh realities to think in certain ways. Our circumstances are almost like a climate that produces certain types of plants. If my mind is the frozen tundra and I want it to be palm trees and tropical fruits, I have to change mind locations and climates. I had to reject maintaining an unchanging "fixed" mindset that leads to stagnation and mediocrity to transition into a "growth" mindset leading to purpose and destiny.

Early on, I learned that this transition doesn't happen because you change careers. You can move from that 9-5 to start your own business, but still have the same fixed mindset. You can become an entrepreneur but still think and work like you used to and get the same results you have always gotten. You have to think and live differently to get different results. Here are a few examples of a growth vs. fixed mindset.

EXAMPLE 1:

Growth: I get it, nobody owes me anything, so I keep it moving.

Fixed: I blame the world for my issues, and I'm mad at the world at times.

EXAMPLE 2:

Growth: I have an opinion, but it may not make sense or be beneficial to share it.

Fixed: I need to share my opinion when I feel strongly and may post it on social media to make my point.

EXAMPLE 3:

Growth: I may hear the gossip (the tea), but I'm not serving it!

Fixed: I listen to all the gossip and share it with others because I enjoy drama.

EXAMPLE 4:

Growth: I go to business conferences with an open mind and willingness to invest in something for self-benefit.

Fixed: I go to business conferences saying, "I hope no one tries to sell me anything!"

EXAMPLE 5:

Growth: Takes risks; likes to be challenged.

Fixed: Plays it safe; doesn't want to be challenged.

EXAMPLE 6:

Growth: I focus on building relationships.

Fixed: I want a quick and easy hook-up.

EXAMPLE 7:

Growth: I try hard, and I keep on trying.

Fixed: I'm not going to keep trying, it's just not working.

EXAMPLE 8:

Growth: I will invest every dime to build my business.

Fixed: I will spend money on everything else, but not nearly enough on my business.

EXAMPLE 9:

Growth: I invested to be in a business mastermind group.

Fixed: I didn't invest in a group, but I share my ideas with friends and family on occasion.

EXAMPLE 10:

Growth: If I network with one person that I can serve, I feel good.

Fixed: I don't connect with anyone here, and I'm not talking to anybody.

So, I ask you. What type of mindset do you have? Growth or Fixed?

It's Painful to See

When I speak at conferences around the world, I can almost immediately see what type of mindset a person has by the way they act, speak, and how they approach me. Growth people are passionate, grateful, and focused on their purpose. Fixed people are distracted, not focused, and often critical of things. They don't realize they are missing the very things they are longing for and need to move forward.

Growth people take notes, connect with people, and make deals all in the same day. They don't care if they are in a penthouse or a basement, if they eat simple snacks or delicious foods. They want knowledge, connections, and don't care where they must go or what they must do to get them. They also begin implementation immediately. They are not overly focused on inconsequential details. They are going somewhere and are convinced they will get there with the right knowledge and connections.

It is amazing how I can predict a person's future success based on their attitude, which reflects their mindset. Growth mindset people see opportunity and are grateful to connect and learn, while fixed thinkers miss so much. It's like 2 people go to an all-you-can-eat buffet with an amazing assortment of food. The fixed mindset person only sees that someone dropped a lemon on the floor by the shrimp cocktail! They miss out on everything because of one small inconsequential issue.

Growth mindsets see great leaders willing to pour into them and that they are surrounded by other entrepreneurs who are determined to make millions. They see people who are creating growth and professional opportunities that MUST be seized! They want to expand their capacity and reach. They look for materials and additional opportunities. They value the trainers, who they are, and what they bring to the table. They attract other growth-minded thinkers.

Fixed mindsets are not flexible or hungry and think everything is a scam. They don't take notes and are distracted by problems or unmet preferences. They miss the value of people, relationships, and atmospheres and so, miss out on what they need. They are focused on limits, roadblocks, and unpleasant realities. They don't care to look at the good. Fixed mindsets see lack and scarcity and in some sick way, are determined to stay stuck. They are determined to be a problem. These are the people who demand refunds, issues chargebacks, and file false Better Business Bureau reports.

Most fixed mindset people are overly passive, but even worse, there are overly toxic and aggressively destructive fixed mindsets. These are the people who make fake pages on social media, hiding behind who they are, and posting negative comments. These are people who purposely try to sabotage you because it makes them feel better. These types of behaviors are not only destructive and unnecessary but highly abnormal! In every situation, you can find good or bad. Fixed mindsets are limited, while growth mindsets are limitless. The choice is yours.

Big Thinkers Won't Deal with Fixed Mindsets!

There are consequences to the way you think. People that make things happen, deliberately avoid fixed mindset people for two reasons. First, they are complainers instead of learners. Secondly, until they change the way they think, they can't receive what someone else has. Therefore, many successful people don't reach back to help others because they have learned that trying to help people that have a fixed mindset is frustrating, draining, and doesn't help them. Don't be that person! Strong leaders only have time for and want to deal with people that get it, who have growth mindsets.

We Must Choose to Lead

I believe that we are all leaders—because, on our life journey, we influence others as we go. The second most important part of your mindset involves leadership. If you cannot lead, then you cannot be successful. All success stems from leadership.

Yet society makes a concerted effort to keep you thinking and behaving like a follower. Everyone from our school teachers to political leaders—even our televisions—tells us who we should be and how we should behave. We are programmed to be like zebras. Let me explain.

The Lion and the Zebra Analogy

We already discussed the two kinds of mindsets—the "fixed or trapped" mindset and the "free and growth" mindset. Both of these tend to represent a follower or leader disposition as well. I have a great analogy to explain them!

Have you ever seen one of those shows where they go to Africa to show all of the beautiful animals and how they interact? One of these scenes is the local waterhole, where a herd of zebras and a pride of lions live close to each other. Both need to exist there to flourish. This is an established system, and both participants, know their roles.

The lions need the water to survive, and so do the zebras. During the winter months, there is lots of water. The zebras' goal is to survive another day. Eat enough grass, drink enough water, and hope they don't get eaten. The lions need to eat the zebras to survive. It is implied that the waterhole is lion territory, not zebra territory. They can claim it whenever they like.

You can liken it to an economy: the working class (poor zebras) and the upper class (wealthy lions). This is how their society functions, even though there are only 14 lions and 600 zebras. At any moment, the zebras could overwhelm the lions, but they do not. The zebras can trample the lions and run free, but instead, they live in survival mode every day. They just want to get enough water and eat enough grass to survive. They live in fear of being eaten but simply hope for the best. The problem is that the zebras will spend their entire life just getting by, but sooner or later, they will get eaten.

This is the picture of the average person working every day. They are afraid of losing their job or the next stock market crash that could ruin them. Then most will enter into retirement hoping to have enough to eat, with many mortgaging their home. Some have nothing left at the ends of their lives, with some families having to do a fundraiser to pay for their funeral expenses! We can live differently if we think differently.

Why do the zebras simply not trample and kill the lions to make life easier? Because they are kept busy from birth—moving from grazing ground to waterhole—and they learn to be terrified of setting a toe away from the herd. If they do, they die. Similar psychology exists in people. We learn to do as we are told and as everyone else is doing. Keep your head down, work hard, and stay busy. Always worry about the water and the lions. You need to break away from the herd if you are going to transition from a zebra to a lion! Lions are intelligent, independent, and territorial. They know that taking command and being a leader within a group of leaders is of the utmost importance to their survival. Which animal do you want to be?

Inaction is the Enemy of Progress

The greatest change agent is action, and the greatest enemy to being a leader is inaction. Think about it, it is impossible to change anything by doing nothing! People are often waiting for some type of magical moment where something mysterious will happen and change everything. As children, we would play pretend and read or watch fairy tales where something or someone comes into the scene and makes everything ok. There are many adults still waiting for someone or something to change everything, and it never comes.

Others are waiting for a special time to come. They put things off and delay with excuses like, "When the kids get out of school at the end of the school year," or perhaps "When the kids start back to school next year." Some people even say, "I'll wait until the start of the New Year," which becomes the Spring or the Fall. This cycle continues over and over again.

It's Now or Never - Your Dreams Can't Wait

I've found that if you don't seize the day, that tomorrow never comes. Or when it does, it's today, and there is some other reason to put it off tomorrow, or next week or next year. You do have today, and you can take action today. If I did not quit my job in 2009 amid a recession, I would not be where I am today. I had to take action; I couldn't sit around waiting for some fairy tale magical moment that would never come.

Don't Wait for Opportunity - Act!

So many people make statements like, "I am going to be successful," and this may be true for some, but you must start something. You have to do something and get things going. One of the differences between me and many others is that I don't wait for opportunity. I push. I fight and kick for the things I want. I create opportunity.

Sometimes I go into things that I can't even see how I will pull it off, but tell myself, that if I can make this happen and get through this, I am one bad chick! When you FIGURE IT OUT and push forward, that's when magical things happen! In Key # 7, I will discuss more about creating opportunities, but for now let's discuss ACTION.

The Difference Between Words and Actions

To be a leader in this world requires heart, courage, and—most of all—action. Action is the one thing that you were taught to fear when you were growing up. DO something wrong, and any number of terrible things could happen.

But words will not get you anywhere unless words are your business. There is a reason why people say, "actions speak louder than words." A true leader knows the difference between imagining and talking—and actually doing something. You get a lot of "fixed" mindset people that talk a big game but never follow through. They want to look smart but avoid challenges and risks, and never intend on exposing themselves to the ridicule of failure. Growth mindset people turn their talk into actions. They don't speak about the same things too often, because there is always progress and something new to talk about. They learn, embrace challenges, and are always reaching for higher levels of achievement in the wake of mistakes and failure.

All brilliant leaders own their words. Words can be very damaging if they keep you doing the same things over and over out of fear. It is your attitude that dictates how you end up behaving. You will often find that once you fully believe that you are a leader, you will begin to act like one naturally. Leaders show other people the way. They encourage the best from those around them. If your mindset is stuck on zebra, you will never grow to the point where you can start turning your deepest desires into reality. Leaders do this on their own despite the risk involved. Lions will not hesitate to pounce at an opportunity. Zebras are always suspiciously eyeing the water, dancing back and forth in fear and thirst.

Actions need to become your new way of thinking about the world. It is how you learn, and as you know, learning is crucial to success. Do not expect to just speak about something and then succeed at it. This is a dream. For dreams to become reality, you have to lay them out—then carefully follow steps that bring them into the real world.

Being the Standard, Setting the Example

Adopting a leadership mindset is also about how you see yourself. Danielle always identified with other hard-working people and never had the confidence to look further than the position just above her, like everything else was unattainable. Her respect for others like her helped ensure that she would "stay the course," which essentially guaranteed a mindset and behaviors where nothing would ever change or improve.

The funny thing about leading is that it is a behavior. The mindset allows you to become the example—no matter what "position" you are in. People are not defined by what they do but by who they are. And I believe that everyone that practices real leadership will be in a better position to act for their success in life.

Leaders do not need to follow someone else's exact example. They can absorb knowledge from multiple sources and become their own example. When people see a leader succeeding, they only see how that individual has caused something great to happen. Then they try and mimic them. They do not see the risk and struggle. Leaders provide the benchmark tests that others are not willing to take.

You need to start so that others can start. Leaders always begin the race—and after them comes everyone else. If we are going to teach success, then you need to take responsibility as a role model. If you step out of the zebra herd and don your lion claws, others will too.

At the same time, Danielle was emulating her superiors, I was aiming much higher learning from people like Oprah Winfrey, Master P, Bill Gates, and Warren Buffett. I did not have the mindset of a follower, so I was able to step out of the herd and reach far beyond my current knowledge to train myself to walk with the authority, confidence, and persona of a leading businesswoman.

Action begins in the mind, so when you assume the identity of a leader, you also assume the actions that a leader is more inclined to take. Leaders will strike out on their own. They will take risks and make incredible things happen. That needs to be you! You cannot hide away in the herd any longer. Be the standard, the benchmark, by altering your mindset. Believe you can lead by leading and learning along the way. Put yourself out there! The alternative is that you will foster a follower mindset, and OTHER people will dictate how your life turns out. Is that what you want?

The Burden of Leadership and Failure

Failure is good—no, it is GREAT for leaders. Followers see failure as an ego-attack, as something so bad that the world will burn around them if it happens. They fail to see the value in learning what NOT to do.

In fact, what NOT to do is exactly how you retrain your mind to succeed. Once you understand the roads you should not take, all that remains are the roads that you should. Again, this is a very basic concept that cripples the general population. If you are afraid of failing, you will never go, and you will never succeed.

There is a lot of burdens that come along with the leadership mindset, sure. You will fail and make tons of mistakes. Hopefully, you will make so many mistakes that you eventually succeed. The only way to truly fail is to quit. Leaders do not quit—they learn, test, reframe, relearn, and test again. They FIND the best success formula.

Failure shapes you as a leader. It is not what you failed at that matters but how you rose up and built that experience into your next successful venture. Everyone fails. But the funny thing about failure is that it teaches you humility. In business, humility can be an incredible asset. It also helps remove the fear of any new situation. So, turning your ideas into actions—then failing—is a critical part of success!

You learn so much when you fail—from others, from yourself, how your mind works, what your challenges and fears are, AND how to overcome them. Failure should never be left on its own. It should be accompanied by the word "overcoming," so put it in context.

You want to be the kind of leader that overcomes failure after failure on your path to success. It is a burden, and people may even lose respect for you along the way. But God knows your heart and what you are trying to achieve. Social vilification has no real effect on you at all. Eventually—when you do succeed—it all comes right.

I find that the more times I fail in business, the better my techniques and skills become. Failing makes me a much, much, better leader. If you can learn to shrug off failing, you can learn to adopt the leadership mindset. One way that people say it is, "I either win or I learn." Failure is not losing; it's learning. So, I either win today or learn so that I can win tomorrow. All leaders fail. If you cannot fail without beating yourself up or wallowing in self-pity for months on end, then you are not a leader. Do not succumb to the tragedy of believing that failing is a NEGATIVE act.

Danielle spent years trying to become good enough to get a small (almost meaningless) promotion. I spent the same amount of time failing and building. I made my first million surrounded by the stigma of failure. Yet I succeeded in the end.

People often say, "You fail your way to the top" or "Learning through failure is the way to success" as a cliché, but I truly believe that failure is one of our greatest teachers. I thought I failed when I was transitioning to my purpose and doing less real estate. Real estate is what built me, but it was never my passion— just a tool to make "money chunks. " All I could think of was that the world was looking at me like I failed.

Failing was scary to me because if I failed, my brand would be tarnished—at least that is what I thought. I started to feel sick doing real estate full-time and I lost the passion for it. Not only that, I started to lose a lot of money because my mind was not in it and my bills became more than I could handle. My office rent alone was $10K monthly. Then there was other overhead, supplies, and staff salaries. I knew I was not making enough to cover it all.

My bills got so out of hand. One time I had to choose between paying my staff salaries or Con Edison, the utility company, who was downstairs ready to turn off my power for nonpayment. These are the choices that entrepreneurs have to make. These are the times when you feel like such a failure. It's embarrassing. But was it really a failure?

Journey of Redirection

As an entrepreneur, I have learned that about every 3-5 years, you should tweak something, morph into something else, or change strategy and direction. What I was going through financially, was showing me it was time. I didn't see it that way at first. All I could see was that my business was failing. But when I look back, I realize that I needed that to happen. My revenue decreasing and my serious lack of passion is what caused me to open my eyes and begin my journey of redirection.

I'm Done

I remember having to make that decision of who I was going to pay, staff salaries or Con Edison, and I said, "I'm done!" I had to be honest that my passion was gone. I realized I had to move on or get stuck in the herd doing the same thing for the next 20 years and be miserable. I realized that it was time to shift and do something different.

I went to my landlord to work out a deal to break my lease two years early because I was sinking. He agreed, and I was so happy because I would have had to pay him about $250K. Then the day I handed over my key, he took me to court the very next day for the $250K! I was broken, I was hurt, and I was financially broke. I was forced to file for bankruptcy, and it was the most humiliating and worst time of my life. After all, at that time, I had been on many television programs, featured in different magazines, and even secured a television show deal with NBC Universal for my very own real estate docuseries, *Powerhouse*. The woman with all of this success is now BANKRUPT!

I was broken to the core and wanted to stay in bed and cry. But it taught me something so powerful. Later it became evident that it was not a failure but a set up for greater things to come that I couldn't see then. It also taught me to never become stagnant in my growth and learning and everything does happen for a reason.

Becoming a Relentless Strategist

There is one thing that leaders do that followers do not do. Leaders tend to record, track, measure, and analyze their past performance. These are all the traits of a relentless strategist. Strategy is applicable in all areas of your life. You cannot deny that when you know where you are going and how to get there, you get there sooner. Now take that concept and apply it to any process. How many ways can I get things done? Which ways work best? This is strategic success.

A great leader is an ever-growing strategist. They see the mistakes that they and others have made in the past, and they actively work to prevent them from happening again. A follower in the same context might say, "What did I do wrong?" They will internalize the failure and take it as a personal affront to their skills and intelligence.

A leader–strategist, on the other hand, will ask, "Where did this go wrong?" They keep the failure separate from who they are and try to find the real reasons for the breakdown. Then they take notes and regroup until they get it right.

- Fail—then move forward.
- Focus on what is important.
- Communicate effectively.
- Assess the strategy that failed.
- Rework the strategy.
- Document everything and make everything measurable.

Danielle focused on improving in her job, while I focused on becoming a better strategist. In the end, my leadership skills were tested dozens of times, and that made me excellent at assessing situations, failing with grace, and getting back on the path of success.

A big part of getting involved in the leadership mindset is letting go of your sense of failure, social perception, and fear. I always told myself that the alternative (being a zebra) would end up destroying my life one day. Remember that sooner or later, all zebras eventually get eaten! Nothing I could do on the path to success ever compared to that undeniable truth.

I would rather spend a lifetime failing as a lion than a single moment succeeding as a zebra. Do you get my point? The real failure is never failing in the first place. I am sure you will agree that there is nothing worse than a constant struggle in this life. I always knew that I was meant for more; I just had to find out what that "more" was. It eventually came to me, and I knew that I had found my purpose. Sometimes in life, there will be so many red flags everywhere that you do not even realize when a white flag rises to show you the way out. The next Key is about building your purpose mindset and knowing exactly who you are in this world.

KEY # 3

Finding Your Passion and Purpose

"There is no passion to be found playing small—in settling for a life that is less than the one you are capable of living."

—Nelson Mandela

One of the prominent secrets to living with an exceptional mindset involves creating passion in your life. Until you put it there, you will not understand how much of an impact adopting a "real" passion can have.

I believe that you have a passion, maybe several of them, lurking beneath the surface in your life. I am going to show you how to bring those passions out and use them to create success.

The Energy of Passion

Passion both brings and requires energy. Forget Red Bull or that next cup of coffee. When you are focused on your passion, your energy level explodes and also endures longer. In your passion, you are fully alive. Your soul screams of joy when you are in your zone and doing what God created you to do. Nobody has to tell, encourage or drive you to follow your passion. Most people won't understand your passion because they don't see what you see or feel what you feel.

The Mundane Diminishes Your Passion

That 9-to-5 you don't like drains you. Those endless bills and that almost negative bank account, they drain you. Living like a zebra hoping to get that next sip of water without having to run for your life drains you. People drama drains you. Many people have lost their focus or passion because they spent the last decade or more being drained trying to survive or not to be a victim.

One thing I learned about lions was that they choose when they fight or kill. They will conserve their energy for when it is needed. They will not be drawn into a fight unless they intend to win. They will not go for a kill unless they are fairly sure they will get it. You never see a lion jogging around tired, thirsty, and frustrated. They are very strategic, but when they pounce or fight, they are very effective. They explode in passion, and they get what they want!

Where Do Your Core Passions Lie?

What if I told you that there are two kinds of passion—the passion that people expect you to have and the one that you genuinely have for a dedicated subject or niche? It is so easy to get the two confused or to limit yourself by trying to make your passion fit into a predefined space that the world has carved out for you. People will constantly encourage you to be passionate about the things they want. This happens every day in the corporate world. It is literally your boss's job to get you to expend your energy on and become passionate about the department or company goals.

Other people will impose something on you because they feel that it is the best fit for you. Let me tell you this now, only you can decide what is and what is not "good" for you. Passion will rise inside your heart when you do what you love most. It will become that driving force that gets you there. Do you know where your core passions lie? Most of the people I have coached say "No" or "Kind of," but owning up to their passion is always a struggle. I think you know that you love something, but when other people disagree with that love or passion, you become intimidated by it.

Passion is a very strong feeling or emotion about an idea, person, or thing that exists inside you. It drives you forward, compels you, and motivates you to continue working towards new ideas in that field. For me, that was running a business, bringing people together in a positive way, and being of service to entrepreneurs.

I Love Bringing People Together

My goal is to reach those people who are where I was when I felt lost and broken. I am passionate about finding those people that are miserable at their

9-to-5 job but have a passion to do something they love. I am passionate about working with those individuals who have a burning desire to win BIG in business and in life. That period of hating my job but loving what I did on weekends taught me so much. I know what it feels like to be stuck and not be doing what you are inspired to do.

For me, loving what I did on weekends wasn't enough. I wanted to do it full-time. I wanted to live my passions and dreams every single day. Being able to do that now, I love it! I love being able to decide how much money I will make this year. I love deciding if I will get up at 5, 6, or 10 in the morning! I love where my passion has brought me, which is essentially freedom.

I always wanted to be a businesswoman. I didn't care what, or how at first, I just wanted to be a businesswoman. I wanted to be creative. I wanted to help people. You cannot be in business if you are not helping someone's problem. I wanted to be that person. The passion was there, my challenge was how I was going to monetize it, and this is something we all have to figure out.

Defining and Executing Your Passions

If you are going to change your mindset and evolve to become a more capable, personally empowered person, you have to outline what your passions are. These are the stepping stones that will help you discover who the "real" you actually is or could be.

I am talking about the passion inside you, the one you might be shying away from because the people around you do not understand it. A young girl from the Bronx had no place in high-end, luxury real estate on Wall Street in New York City, but I had a real passion for business—and this allowed me to break through the stigma surrounding it. I set out to prove everyone wrong, and I did. You can too!

"One day" is the enemy of passion and an imaginary time that never comes. Have you ever noticed how you plan to "one day" pursue your passion? In the meantime, you have to live every day working in a job that you do not enjoy. It is a horrible way to live.

That is why I would encourage you and every other person I meet to sit down and outline the passion that drives you forward. A passion-driven lifestyle is naturally goal-focused because you are always on the way to the next level. When you do not live a passion-driven life, you end up floating in limbo. Limbo is a terrible place to be in your life because when good things happen, they do not make you as happy; when bad things happen, you accept them as "normal." Everything is gray, and advancement stops. No one wants to live a gray life. That is why you have to outline the things you are passionate about.

- **What are your core or fundamental values?** These are the main beliefs that you live by; your passion cannot conflict with these.
- **What is it that you love to do?** When everything else is done, what do you choose to work on when you have the time?
- **Combine your core values and the things that you love to do.** Are there careers or a business you can start that contain both of these things?

Before facing what your passion might be, consider this—we all have talents. Passion may be associated with your talents, but it does not have to be directly linked to them. You could have a real passion for cars, for example, and never have changed the oil in one.

Outlining the passion that drives you is very important. If you do not have something that pushes you forward and provides extra motivation for you daily, you will not be able to reach those levels of greatness that you deserve.

That saying, "Do what you love, and you will never work a day in your life" is about passion. It implies that if you can work hard in a field that you are passionate about, success will happen, but it won't feel like work. I came to believe this universal truth after discovering my natural knack for business.

Talents and Passion Often Go Hand in Hand

Although I am passionate about what I am doing in business, coaching people, and doing events for entrepreneurs, I am also good at it! Some of these things are just gifts from God. It is how He made me and whatever God made you for, you will be both passionate and good at doing. But we still have to act, train, learn, and build.

So many people can sing but don't sing, others can draw but don't draw. I find it so hard to believe that people have talents, but once again, so many people who have great talents simply don't know how to monetize it. Too many dream, but don't act on their dream. They let their gifts, talents, and passion lay stagnant.

I also want to add that this type of "dreaming" is dangerous. When you reach the point where your dreams are so old that they have passed into "wishful thinking," these can damage your self-confidence and prevent you from even starting out on your road to success. A dream is just a dream—it is what "could" have happened in your life. There is only who you are now, your passion, and the opportunity to find out how far you can go if you put passion at the center of your life.

As a strategic thinker, I am always brainstorming new ways to become more efficient at what I do. It is a skill that has served me well in my life and one that I would like to pass onto you before you set out on your journey to discovering your authentic passion. You see, even once you have worked through ALL the opposition (your passion vs. what people believe should be your passion), you will still need to practice this passion every day so that you can be consistent in your goals.

Now, this is not easy. Even the top businesspeople in the world struggle with being consistently passionate about things. That is why I like to build a plan around "practicing passion" and integrate that with my daily schedule. You can do it too.

You should already have a list of your passions. Now write down how often you nurture or spend time on these. Practicing passion means taking your powerful interest in that thing, adding it to a schedule, and enjoying every second that you spend immersed in it. Your plan should consist of practicing your passion for at least a few hours every day. If your goal is to eventually do your passion full-time, you are never going to get there if you cannot make some time for it now.

When you invest time in something, it stimulates more interest in that area. Every time I learned something new about business, I grew hungrier to learn more. If I distracted myself with other things, it became harder to practice my passion. You need to include your passion in your life every day without fail. Your plan should contain what your passions are and how you can successfully practice them. When you make time for yourself like this, the returns are incredible. Make sure that your passion becomes a part of your daily life.

- Passion is acknowledging that you have strong feelings for certain niche areas, things, or people. This feeling will NOT always be strong.
- Do not confuse passion with motivation; passion should inspire you, but it is a practice. If you do not practice it, do not expect to stay motivated by it.

You must find and nurture your passion. The equation looks like this: **CURIOSITY + ENGAGEMENT x TIME = PASSION**. This is how passion is built and maintained. Like going to the gym, you can expect results from the work you put in, but if you neglect the work, those same muscles you build up will diminish. You must build your passion. Once you have found your niche, it will change to look like this: **PASSION + TIME x MOTIVATION = RESULTS**. Work always comes before results. Passion, skill, and time can work together powerfully to get the results you are after and deserve!

Passionate, Not Passive Mindset

There are active mindsets and passive mindsets; I mentioned this earlier in the book when I gave you the lion and the zebra analogy. But there is something here that I want you to think about in greater detail.

Activity is something that is inspired because there is a very strong emotional bond that you have with an end goal. You might decide to bake a chocolate cake because you want to do something nice for your brother, who is celebrating a birthday. The end goal of doing something nice out of love is what drives you to bake that cake.

In the same way, passion drives all activities in your mind. It is a passion mindset that you should foster so that you can approach all of your goals with a fiery determination that will blow people away. Focused intensity always produces greater results than monotonous repetition. Remember the lion's focused intensity results in the fight won or that next meal.

It is so easy to accept that "stuff" happens to you in your life that you can forget that you have the power to make positive things happen as well. A passive mindset watches, waits, and accepts when the time comes. A passion-driven, active mindset assesses and identifies opportunities and takes action according to a preset timeline.

Let me be clear—anything is achievable when you are driven by enough passion. That is why you need to spend time in that area. It is the one thing that will motivate you to be persistent with your goals. This may be a total mindset shift from how you operate right now.

You have to stop believing that there will be some time in the future when things will "work out" and get better. By the time you realize that they will not, you are older, and worse off. Too many people spend their lives hoping or wishing for change that never comes. A few years ago, the statement, "Be the change you are looking for," became popular because it takes passionate ownership that is experienced.

- **A passion mindset** works towards a positive future by practicing passion every day and moving forward with real goals that are broken down into small, achievable steps.
- **A passive mindset** works toward a negative future by ignoring time constraints, excusing away motivation, and leaving things to chance so that they will never get done or materialize.

You see, it is not that you are doing nothing—you are actually practicing a negative mindset, which is forcing you closer to a negative outcome. You need to sort this out now so that you can stop sabotaging your dreams. One of the harsh realities of life is that effort does not guarantee results, especially desired results. It is up to you to push for results and be persistent.

The Strength Behind Persistence

There is real strength behind persistence and the ability to maintain it over certain periods of time. That is what separates highly successful people from everyone else. Going from a lazy mindset to a persistent one is challenging, but persistence can be learned and established through discipline. Most people don't talk or think like this, but those who achieve greatness live in this type of mind space.

Persistence behaves like the battery in your car. When it is on, the car moves forward. When it is off, the car stands stationary. The question then becomes—how do I make sure that I am always persistent? By adding fuel to your car! That fuel is called motivation.

When was the last time you felt compelled to do something? Perhaps it was cleaning your house, going food shopping or starting a business. The concepts are really the same—the formula just needs to be applied to the less obvious areas of your life. For example, you have to persistently buy food because food keeps you alive. This creates a set need or motivation for you to get down to the shop and buy some groceries. You never have a problem doing this because there is a very clear understanding of your need: **NO FOOD = STARVATION AND DEATH.**

In the same way, you have to realize that when you work with persistence and motivation, they will only work if you have a very clearly defined need that you understand to be entirely non-negotiable. You would never procrastinate about food because it is crazy to entertain the idea that you can go without it for even one day.

The same strength needs to be applied when it comes to your passion-based objectives. The only way you will ever truly succeed is if you can understand that need is equal to (maybe even greater than) your need for food. Motivation is the fuel that keeps the persistent fire burning inside you. The only way to stay motivated is to continue to practice motivation.

A motivated and persistent person always has energy and is eager to learn, which of course inspires more learning and practice, which translates into personal development. To find out if you are motivated and persistent, think about your average day.

- **What do you get done on your average day?**
- **What do you get done on a highly productive day?**
- **What do you get done on a slow, unproductive day?**

Persistence requires flawless application and is decidedly one of the most difficult traits to adopt. Knowing what your current mindset is like will help you avoid the pitfalls.

Being Persistent Like a Bee on Honey

Persistence in life is born from motivation, as I have mentioned. Once you are actively practicing motivation, you will naturally become more persistent. I like the old me, but I like the new me better! I like being able to look in the mirror and see my "persistence muscles" that have been built. You, too, can raise your persistence levels as well.

To become an absolute persistence wizard, you will need to nurture the following types of mindset and practice:

- Become really good at guessing accurate timelines. Persistence can get derailed if you underestimate how long something is going to take you, so become well versed in the art of time estimations so that your deadlines, timelines, and goals can be met.

- Keep your motivation firmly in mind. You will always need to answer the question "why," so keep your motivation close, and practice it when you need to.

- If you fail, dust yourself off and get back to work! Being persistent means that you can overcome any setbacks and get on with your original goals. Your first idea did not work? Fine, move on to the next one. Many of the most successful businesspeople in history failed dozens of times. They did not let it stop them!

- Call time outs or take breaks to assess and make adjustments. If you watch sporting events, a good coach calls a time-out when momentum shifts to break negative momentum, adjust, and gain positive momentum. In a boxing match, if a boxer has a bad round, between rounds, he rests, gets advice and encouragement, and then goes out to win the next round.

- Find other equally persistent people. Join forces and enjoy success together. When you have positive people around you, you can encourage and motivate each other to heights you never believed possible.

- Focus on minimizing your stress levels. When you stress about everything, life goes by in a blaze of colors. When you are moving too fast, you make mistakes, get frustrated, and do not give it your best. Slow down, stay calm, and think about the things you do and the decisions that you make.

I taught myself how to be persistent like a bee on honey. Bees are attracted to all things sugary, but honey most of all. They spend all of their time focused on that honey and how they are going to create it. That means long hours sourcing the best pollen from the brightest flowers. When they are done, they bring it back to the hive, and the worker bees start the process. Without the persistence to continually seek out pollen for honey creation, the bees would starve in the leaner months when there are no available flowers.

You have to learn how to reset your mind so that it works like a bee that is constantly motivated to find pollen to create honey. Persistence will lead you to the point where, like the honey, you have enough financial wealth to see you through the leaner months. Remember, like a muscle, persistence must be built and maintained.

How to Get Motivated

How am I ever going to get motivated when I feel lost, I'm sad, my money is funny, and I'm miserable at times? These might be the questions that pop into your head. The key is not to worry; the practice exists and has existed all along. There are literally dozens of different mindset strengthening techniques that you could use to help you foster motivation in your life.

- **Begin with an end goal in mind.** You have to have a destination if you are going to program your internal GPS! Otherwise, you could head off on a thousand different paths and never get to where you need to be.
- **Once you have that solid, firm goal in mind, visualize it.** Create a mental picture of that outcome and imagine what you would feel when it happens.
- **Grab your notebook and write down a long list of reasons why you desperately need to accomplish that goal.** Break the goal down into smaller pieces so that they are completely manageable in your life.

- **Follow the GPS.** Once you have your goals (the destination) and your method of achieving them (direction), you will feel much more inspired and motivated to get it done. This is because your brain can now see exactly how long it will take to achieve and what the journey will entail.

Motivation is not something that jumps out at you. It is not some thrilling rush of adrenaline that seizes you and makes you super-productive. Essentially, motivation is about three core concepts.

- **The first is presence.** Motivation needs to be something you consciously think about all the time. The trick to being motivated is to know that you have to be motivated.

- **The second is practice.** Motivation has to be practiced every single day in real ways. That means before you engage in an activity, you need to stop, acknowledge your motivation for what you are about to do, and then do it.

- **The third is proof.** Motivation thrives on reward because it lets your subconscious mind know that you are heading in the right direction. Goal achievement feeds your motivation and urges you onward.

Practicing motivation can consist of reading books that inspire you, hanging powerful quotes on your wall, leaving reminders for yourself in strategic locations, and referring to a vision board. I will tell you all about mine in Key #5. For now, nurturing motivation in your life will be the fuel that allows the engine of persistence to run—and it will take you to your chosen destination, whatever that may be.

Not Giving in to Procrastination

You have to train yourself to be a non-procrastinator. It is so easy to get caught up in your own life and the lives of those around you that you often forget that entire months or even years go by—and you are not getting closer to your ultimate goals. I heard a saying that, "Procrastination is the thief of time." This is so true! It is so easy to sit down to work only to be distracted by social media, email, phone calls, and other things that do not serve you.

I have learned that procrastination is a choice like anything else in life. When you do not have a clear direction—and a goal to match—procrastination is the result. It is your job as an individual with a strong mindset to overcome this lingering result.

I like to apply Newtonian science in my everyday life because it clarifies things for me. Newton was the genius who discovered gravity and the laws of cause and effect. According to Newton, procrastination is a result of something. It is either a cause or an effect; it is either an action or a reaction. When you put it in context, you can figure out why it exists in your life. Is your procrastination a result of your lack of planning? Have you set goals to counteract it? Is procrastination the result of spending too much time away from your passion?

I understood early on that procrastination was going to be a constant adversary in my life. I had a propensity for it, and I knew that it was not in my best interest. The only way I was ever going to leap over the procrastination hurdle was if I filled all of that empty space with something. So, I filled it with practicing my passion. Instead of practicing procrastination (which is what we do most often), I scheduled away all of the "empty" time that was holding me back. It worked!

That is why I would encourage you to never give in to procrastination. It is the single most dangerous thing that will keep your mind lazy, your hands idle, and your dreams stagnant. Even if you work on your passion for 20 minutes every day, after a month, that is 600 minutes or 10 hours that you get to spend working on your passion every month. That's 120 hours a year or 3 full work weeks. How much can you get done if you were totally focused on a 3-week project? It may take that one year to experience the growth and achievements to prepare you for bigger moves, but it is time well invested and achievable by anyone! And do not forget, when you practice your passion, you are actively staying away from practicing procrastination!

Making Time for Your Passions

Many people are bogged down working 40 or 80 hours a week! On top of that, there is the commute, cooking dinner, the children, and endless other things that eat away our time. If you are ever going to exercise your passions, you must set hours dedicated to what you are passionate about. You may work a 9-to-5, and those 8 hours are dedicated to your job, but you must also set office hours for the things you are passionate about. In the same way, you stick to your 9-to-5, you have to stick to your 7-to-9 hours or Saturday 12-to-2 hours of passion activities whatever they may be. You have to inject that into your lifestyle and stick with it. This is non-negotiable because our passions are so intertwined with our purpose.

An Exercise in Time Management

So far, you understand that motivation fuels persistence and that it is beneficial for you to involve other people in that process so that you reach your end result much like bees do. But there is a third element to this mindset equation—time! If you can master how you use time in your life, you can seize control of your schedule and make the most amazing things happen. "I do not have time" is the silliest, worst thing I hear people say when I speak across the country. There is ALWAYS more time in your day if you know where to look. If there is not another spare moment, then your time to value ratios are horribly off. It can only be one or the other. Most people have every moment of their life booked, just on the wrong things. You cannot work extremely hard all day for nothing.

Time management is about dedicating goals for every hour of your day. Get it on your side, and you will eliminate procrastination and task-avoidance once and for all. You will not have to worry about anything because you can design your ideal life in hours.

- **Time management is not only about scheduling work.** It is also about scheduling in the things that matter such as rest, hobbies, relationship time, social time, family time, and whatever else is most important to you.

- **You can focus on "project" weeks, which makes scheduling easier.** Pick one project that you want to achieve in the space of a week and get to it. Before you know it, that week will be over, and you will be one step closer to your goals.

- **Aim for a 50% time split.** Half of your life should be dedicated to working, and the other half to things that keep you stable and happy enough to perform well while working.

- **Avoid Distractions** like your phone, email, social media, friends, and family if it does not contribute to getting your task done. If you know that you need a break to clear your head and want to do something that is not so productive, schedule it in! You deserve breaks—but not for too long!

Becoming better at time management can get easier. All you have to do is start and then use the previous tactics to never stop. These will keep your schedule moving in the right direction. You must not start a day without a completed schedule, or you will lose hours to procrastination and "nowhere land." Wasting time is not something that helps your life, and yet it is a habit most of us need to break before we can become productive.

How Much Is Your Hour Worth?

I often ask people, "What is your hourly rate?" Based on that rate, what are some things you should NOT be doing or that you should pay someone else to do? For instance, people don't understand the value of a housekeeper. I have had housekeepers for years, simply to free up my time to make money. I am not talking about the most expensive housekeeper, but someone that I could afford who can clean my house, so I can spend my time earning more money.

This speaks to the personal value that you put on your time and skill set. How many mundane or non-productive activities are you engaged in? If you can pay someone $40 to mow your lawn so you could make $300-$500 on a project, why wouldn't you do that? Why don't you sit down and make a list of items you could delegate or hire someone to do? You may be surprised that this could easily be 10-20 hours per week. How much revenue could you produce with these extra hours? How much is your hour worth?

Shifting Your Mindset and Searching for Your Greater Purpose

Without a solid purpose, the entire mindset chain weakens and breaks. You cannot set your direction without a clearly defined destination. Your purpose is that destination. To begin, you will need to look inside yourself. I believe that each one of us has a personal mission in this world, given to us by God. No one can tell you what that is, but you can find out for yourself.

Your purpose is made up of the things that you love to do, the things you are incredibly good at doing, and the projected legacy that you want to leave behind one day when you pass on. I have met some people who have no idea what their purpose might be and some who seem to have dozens of different potential purposes.

I believe that there is one main purpose for everyone. If it feels like you have several, it may be because your unique purpose will involve you using all of the skills and talents that you have at a future point. I also believe that it is impossible for you not to have a purpose. Everyone exists for a reason; you are God's creation. While only you and God may know what that purpose is, it is up to you to communicate it to others and live it.

I found that I prayed a lot during those tough days when I was starting my business. I spent a lot of time soul-searching and reaching out to God to ask Him to keep me on the right path. This faith is what made up any shortfall between my ability to motivate myself and persist, and the adversity I was up against.

You are never alone when you go through these trial periods in your life; God is always there—use Him! He wants to be involved, and He wants to help you. To discover your purpose, you may have to take some difficult roads to get there. If you do not try, you will never know.

Leaving it up to chance is no longer a prospect for you. The outcome of chance is exactly what scared me away—the limited time for life, the terrible financial restrictions, and the crushing poverty at the end in retirement. In life, there is a type of gravity that constantly pulls us into mundane, unproductive, and wasteful activities. To overcome gravity, a stronger force must be implied, and that force is purpose which is fueled by passion and persistence!

From my lessons on the road to my purpose, I can tell you that it is NEVER too late to look inside yourself and reach out to God for help. Together you can find your ultimate purpose, and when you unite it with the other mindset skills you have learned in this book so far, it will change your life. I know because it changed mine.

I learned that discovering your purpose should be your default purpose—at least until it becomes incredibly clear which direction your life is heading in. When you aim to discover what your destination is, it becomes a goal—and goals can be attained.

So, you see—you have no excuse! Even if you cannot conceive of a life purpose for yourself right now, that is okay. It is perfectly normal. For now, your default will be set to "Find out my life purpose." To begin, you will need to face some questions about who you are and what you want out of life. If you can do that, then you will slowly see patterns forming.

- **Your life can be anything you want it to be.** So, what do you want it to be? Take a moment and outline your ideal life. It does not have to be the life of a billionaire but make it realistic and the most ideal version of what you want from the world.

- **Dedicate yourself to consistent learning.** Your greatest tool is relentless learning. Learn from experts. Read books, attend conferences, seminars and workshops. Listen to podcasts and talk about life changing principles and practices with other like-minded passionate people. If you are a trumpet player, invest in the best instrument, learn the history, go to seminars and take private lessons. If your goal is starting a business, learn from entrepreneurs through seminars and online. Invest in a proven business coach. Network with people both locally and from other cities. Take action! Do NOT be passive or wait for others to learn or attend these events with you.

- **Think about the people and places in your life.** These make up very important parts of your world. Decide who you would ideally want in your life and where you would all be. What would it take to get there?

You can see where I am going with this. To secure lasting purpose, you have to implement actions—just like you did with motivation and persistence. In your journey to self-discovery, you cannot be afraid to try new things, make mistakes, or head down the wrong paths. Sometimes you have to jump on board with something working for someone else until you find your purpose.

People that are afraid never start walking. A journey cannot be taken if you do not literally step out of your comfort zone and take the first step. You have already started with this book, and I hope it inspires you to find a deeper level of understanding within yourself. Lasting purpose is just that—purpose that lasts a lifetime. Once you have it, it will never go away. That single driving force will become your life's work and the legacy that you leave behind one day when you are gone.

The growth mindset will take you down many roads, but only one leads to your ultimate purpose—your reason for being born into this world. Find it! The earlier, the better. You have to search to find what your purpose is in this world. Pick a route and go with it, and if you are heading in the right direction, there will be signs along the way; you will have to be ready to act.

The Inner Workings of Discipline and Willpower

Everything in life is connected. If you are going to find your purpose, then you will need to work on two skills that will facilitate this process: discipline and willpower. Without these two practices, you will not be able to reach your ultimate purpose.

- **Choose to be disciplined.** Practice it, and eventually, you will form the habit of being a disciplined person. This is how you can change your self-perception to overcome "laziness" and stick to your schedules.

- **Choose to practice willpower.** Train yourself to make the right decisions when opportunities come. For example, you may need to work, but your friends may want to do something unproductive. You will need the willpower to say NO!

Your life is made up of many decisions. From when to get up, to what to cook, what to wear, and how hard to work—each tiny little decision is made in your conscious mind and affects your life. The process of realizing your purpose is the hardest thing in the world to do—let's get that straight. Very few people realize their potential and fulfill their purpose. That said, YOU are the only person standing in your way.

The inner workings of each of these decisions have far-reaching consequences. An average life is a result of making average decisions. An exceptional life is the result of making the right decisions most often, even if you make some bad decisions on the journey.

You must shape your mind into a lean, mean, highly disciplined machine so that you can exercise willpower when it counts—and it ALWAYS counts. It will take daily practice and thousands of micro-decisions to create your life and reach your ultimate purpose. Always remember, you are NOT a product of your circumstances, you are a product of YOUR decisions.

Ready yourself for change because that is the only constant in the world. Your life will be different in five years' time. You might as well imagine the best version of it, then work tirelessly towards that purpose or vision.

- **Discipline** your mind so that it works for your benefit and not against you. It is NOT okay to be lazy, and it is NOT okay to procrastinate and waste time.

- **Practice willpower** whenever you get the opportunity by making consciously positive decisions that will benefit you in life.

- **Inch closer** towards your purpose by acknowledging that your actions, your level of discipline, and your overall willpower matter. Be firm with yourself; no one will care more than you do.

Understanding Your Individual Journey

Everyone on this planet has an individual journey that they have to take alone. This is your life. It can be frightening and scary to realize that you cannot rely on anyone else to live it for you, but there you go. That is what life is—the slow realization that you get out what you put in.

God wants you to lead a purpose-driven life, but he leaves you the choice. If you read the Bible enough times, it is pretty clear that everything is motivated by choice. Right now, the world has a very large population of people that exist on default—that is, the setting that makes them oblivious to how they live their own lives.

If you live life on default (like everyone else), then you will end up just like them. You need to live life differently. Again, no one can tell you how. I can only teach you what it means to change your mindset and align it in a way that will help you make the right decisions about your life.

At the end of the day, you still have to make those choices, however. All choice is a double-edged sword and can take you to different places. Your goal in this life is to make enough good choices that your purpose is fulfilled.

- **Spend more time with yourself, exploring your spirituality and inner self.** There is real truth to be found when you explore who you are from the inside out.

- **Adopt a love of learning and choose to learn with every lesson.** Limit how often you repeat the same mistakes, and you will move forward.

- **Many paths lead to your purpose.** The trick is to be on one of them. When you do nothing and spend your life working and surviving, you cannot live. Then you are in the wilderness, not on the path.

- **Create momentum in your life by practicing what people seem to believe are inherent traits—things like motivation, persistence, choice, willpower, and discipline.** These can all be practiced and adopted.

- **Pursue your purpose with love and a view to helping others do the same.** I often find that life can be at its most rewarding when you help others reach the same point as you. This is an incredibly rewarding way to live.

To understand your individual journey may take the rest of your life. The goal is to know that it is all driven by your mind, how it works, and the attitudes that you adopt towards the choices that you make on a micro and macro scale. It will not always be an easy journey, and you will have to endure many challenges, however, you MUST keep going. Now, let's talk about these challenges in Key #4, and how to overcome them.

KEY # 4

Overcoming Challenges

"In the depth of winter, I found there was, within me,
an invincible summer."

—Albert Camus

I believe that everyone writes their own life story, whether they intend to or not. Often when you live in poverty, extreme social misalignment can weigh on you, anchoring you to a place you do not want to be. As you strengthen your free mindset, it becomes your responsibility to adjust so that you can start thinking like a person of influence and means. Being stuck in the "poverty" mindset does nothing for you!

Overcoming the Weight of Poverty

You indeed become what you worry most about during your average day. If you constantly stress about paying bills and making ends meet, you will never solve the overriding problem, which is that you do not earn enough money! I found on my journey that overcoming the weight of poverty was a huge lesson. I was expecting to step out of having nothing into a world of shiny new things, opportunities, and freedom. What I found was more responsibility, increased pressure, and a real understanding of the true cost of poverty.

You cannot afford to be poor or to live with the "poverty" mindset: "Every day is a struggle," "I never have enough money," or "I cannot seem to afford anything or make enough to cover all of my debt." If you have thought of any of the previous statements, you may be afflicted with the "poverty" mindset. I call it this because it traps you inside a world of poverty, and it forces you to see your life from the viewpoint that you have nothing, and that life is a battle. It makes every experience a struggle, and that causes your outlook to become negative.

Being raised in the Bronx, I was constantly reminded of "lack" and how "limited" resources were because we had very little. Even though we lived like this, I didn't realize it until I got older. This is what happens to people who are part of a system. We tend to accept things as the norm—when you don't know better, you don't expect better.

Growing up, I went back and forth between my father and mother's homes. My mother's home was more of a family environment where we celebrated the holidays like Thanksgiving and Christmas, and we had tons of food. We were on food stamps, so food was never our issue, but there was dysfunction in my family dynamic. My family fought a lot, but to me, this was all normal. I remember just flowing with all of this as I grew up and didn't think much about it.

When I was mad at my mother, I went to my dad's house, which was a little better because he was an entrepreneur and had a little more money. He lived in a building where he had an apartment, and me and my brothers had another apartment even when we were as young as 10-years-old. He lived down the hall, but we still had to learn how to survive on our own—cook, clean, even go food shopping.

I didn't know if we were doing good or bad. I knew we weren't rich, but I didn't see that we were terrible. So, I felt our circumstances were normal because I didn't know any better. I am grateful that I was able to push through that because many I grew up with never did. They never escaped the poverty of life or got out of poverty-stricken neighborhoods.

Poverty traps your mind! To overcome this crushing way of thinking, you really have to fight against poverty in your life. When you think like a poverty-stricken person, you are always worried about saving, scraping by, reorganizing money, just making it, and getting by. This, my friends, is no way to live. Focusing on "survival" is not a life; it is a punishment. You will often find that the people who escape this mindset do so by focusing their energies on being positive and seeing the good in the world.

Choosing Positivity Over Negativity

Every day is a new opportunity to choose positivity over negativity. When you focus your mind on the positive things in your life, it creates abundance wherever you go. However, this is a learned mindset.

You may not even realize the far-reaching effects of your current negative mindset. I am here to tell you that it is time to question and replace this negative mindset that is holding you back. With negativity comes limitation, fear, and inactivity. If you can change that to a positive outlook, you will create opportunity, progress, and activity in your life.

- **Negative** people are obsessed with what they do not have, and they constantly think about worst-case scenarios, sickness, bankruptcy, and struggle. It is impossible to succeed when you are convinced that at any moment, you will fail.
- **Positive** people are obsessed with what they do have, and they constantly think about the future, best-case scenarios, gratitude, happiness, and their next big achievement. It is impossible to fail when you are convinced that at any moment you will succeed.

Do you see the differences in the way people think? A positive mindset is about so much more than choosing to see life from a new perspective. It is about acknowledging that what your mind focuses on it manifests. It is a universal truth that if you look everywhere for negative results, you will always find them. The same goes for positive results. The choice has and always will be up to you. One small, well-placed positive thought can launch an empire—I believe that.

When things really started changing in my life, I noticed a huge shift in my attitude. Not only was I practicing a positive mindset, but along the way, I was proving to myself that being positive works—because good things were happening all around me. No matter how hard I struggled (and I really did sometimes), my mindset pulled me through it. I think, as people that live with very little, we are reminded about life's scarcity and how cruel life can be. Along the way, we are battered and marginalized until things feel hopeless.

When things are bad, you may forget to choose to be positive. Being positive can be hard when the world is crumbling around you. Those who choose to reject negativity and embrace positivity will win. Those who choose to reject the "victim" mindset and focus on a positive outlook on life will attract money and success.

Rejecting Your Victim Mindset

Have you ever heard of the victim mindset? It has always been associated with negativity and poverty and is probably the reason why you have not been able to rise above your circumstances until now. Let's be honest. Society does not reward people that think outside of the box and want to be personally responsible for their lives. It is built on a culture of non-responsibility, where your life is a result of decisions other people have made. You might blame your parents, your friends, your education, or your spouse, but the reason why you may be struggling is never directed where it should be—at you. A victim allows things to happen to them, no matter what they are.

Victim mindsets accept that bad things are everywhere, and they spend their lives preparing for the bad because it is coming. When you believe "bad things always happen to you," you adopt a victim mindset. Victims cannot be successful because they cannot be responsible.

Well, I say, "Reject your victim mindset right now!" Do not surrender your personal power to your circumstances or environment. The first step is realizing that the victim mindset is something that is encouraged and imposed on you. The next step is to reject it! YOU are responsible for your life, your surroundings, and how much you have or do not have. No excuses, no blame, and no negativity. If you are poor, negative or struggling—YOU are the reason! Accept responsibility for your problems even if you do not feel it is your fault. Once you accept responsibility, you can become a weapon for change. Claim personal responsibility for your life, and you can and will change it for the better. It is that simple.

The opposite of the victim mindset is the active conqueror mindset. ALL successful people are active conquerors, building success in their lives, and overcoming obstacles daily. People like that NEVER give in to negativity. I am proud to say that I am an active conqueror! When I want something, I plan, work it out, and then get it. Since I am not weighed down by what I do not have and what I cannot do, I am free to forge ahead and create my own reality.

Rejecting the victim mindset is a big one. Once you change the way you view yourself, your world, and the things that happen to you in it, you will never be the same—and that is the best thing you can do for yourself—reclaim responsibility for your life. You are not a victim!

How to Break Through Any Obstacle

Obstacles are what make life worth living. A negative person views them with fear, apprehension, and suspicion, while a positive person sees them as another opportunity to attain greater levels of success. You need to become the kind of person who can overcome and break through any obstacle. With the right mindset, this is not only possible but a "must" if you are going to stay on your success path.

Danielle would always talk to me about her problems at work, but she would never take steps to eliminate the problem. They would just become part of her daily life and another "stressor" in her environment. With me, on the other hand, I was geared towards problem-solving. If a problem existed, I wanted to figure out how to get it out of my way.

- I would begin by **emptying my mind of negative nonsense.** By embracing the problem, I could consider it from all angles.
- Once my positive mind was fully engaged, I would outline the problem— **see the goal and focus on setting an achievable target.**
- Using various tools, I would then **envision myself overcoming the obstacle** and completely succeeding in my chosen, outlined goal.
- After this, I concentrated my energy on completing that goal by **setting a realistic but challenging deadline** for myself.
- I would proceed until I reached the goal. **I did not slow down, and I did not give up.** The entire time I believed I was overcoming my obstacles until it was done.

No matter what kind of obstacle I have had to face in the past, I have always been able to overcome it with these steps. You have to start focusing your positive mind on the right area, adding in strategic planning, and then executing your plan until you secure a successful result. When you are satisfied the obstacle is gone, you can move on.

When you become someone who can overcome anything, doors open up for you. The basic formula: **FOCUS + SET GOALS + WORK HARD +**

BELIEVE IN YOURSELF = SUCCESS. People that don't believe this are stuck in a negative mindset, and cannot make it work, because they have no sense of self-responsibility. Most of what holds you back in life come from your mind. Mental barriers stop you from taking the first step on many potentially successful journeys.

As I was growing up and learning to reject what society had for me, I looked and thought about the people around me, and no one had a success formula. I looked at some of my family, and it seemed like no one cared. No one even talked about anything related to entrepreneurship or making millions. My father was the closest thing to anything entrepreneurial, selling records on the street. This was my only glimpse of what it took to run a business. No one else had any vision beyond getting a job. People wanted to go to school and work. I never heard anyone dream about goals, building things, and what they wanted to do next.

This saddens me because decades later, those same relatives (and friends) are still in the same place, doing the same thing. I don't want to impose feelings and say they are miserable, but honestly, I cannot see how they can be happy. I can't see or understand how you can be happy living in the same building for 25 years, literally driving the same car and staying at the same or even less pay for 25 years!

Many will argue it's not about the material, but we need material! We need things, and we get to choose what those things will be. Why wouldn't someone want nice things that make you comfortable and happy? If making the same amount of money, living in the same place, and driving the same car makes you happy, I am not talking to you. I am talking to that person who wants more out of life and doesn't want to live in poverty or even mediocrity.

I grew up in the Bronx, New York, but I'm sorry (not sorry) to say that there are some parts of the Bronx that I cringe at when I visit. I don't understand how people live there or even go to the corner store. It's not for me! I cringe and I'm NOT comfortable at all. Yes, I was born and raised in the Bronx, NY, some of my family still lives there. Yes, to a degree, I do represent the Bronx—It is where I'm from, it made me who I am today. However, when I leave this earth, PLEASE DO NOT BURY ME IN THE BRONX...just saying! Yes, I said it! Now let's move on to Key # 5!

KEY # 5

Your Internal Power

"You never know how strong you are until being strong is the only choice you have."

—Bob Marley

An open mind with the ability to embrace and exercise your personal internal power is the greatest tool that you can have as a human being. Contrary to popular belief, expressing your personal power is not easy. It takes discipline, motivation, and practice to train your mind on success all the time. It was a lesson I had to learn, and one I strongly encourage you to learn early, too.

The Map to Success Is in Your Mind

Everyone is born with different skills, talents, and ways to become richer and more successful. The map to success for every individual is always inside their mind. What I mean by this, is that you need to train your mind to act for the benefit of your life. How can your mind take action, you ask? By focusing on the right things and spending enough time aligning your thoughts with your goals on your average day. When you can always see your endpoint, you run a little faster to get there.

So, your success, as it stands, is locked away in your mind. If you are anything like me, you will need to work consistently at it to unleash it on the world. That means changing your mind by using several modern conditioning techniques. A mind that is changed and trained to be more successful, more positive, and more practical will almost always find a way to excel. I believe that your personal map to success is locked away in your mind right now—and that we just need to get it out.

- Start by **learning more about life**. How does it work? Why does it work that way?

- Understand that your mind is unique. **No one in the world thinks, feels, or behaves as you do.** This is a huge asset, but it can also be a weakness.

- Dedicate yourself to expressing your internal personal power by

unlocking the power of your mind and documenting how the change happens on your journey.

- Even if you are not someone that journals, I would suggest getting one; it will help you notice how your thoughts change and when the **scales start tipping in your favor.**

The best part about this journey is the realization that you are more capable than you ever dreamed possible. These exercises will help you recognize and embrace that.

The Incredible Power of Affirmations

I bet you know what affirmations are, but your mindset has prevented you from seeing their true potential. Affirmations are those short, powerful statements that you can say that help instruct your subconscious mind using conscious conditioning.

If I want to start believing that something is true, I can create an affirmation for it—and then start using it every day. Eventually, my mind will come to see it as the truth, and it will affect my belief systems. Once those belief systems are altered, your actions change and begin to reflect the affirmation that you have been using.

Remember, the only barrier is your mind. Affirmations make it easier to change your belief systems so that they support and align with your goals. You can work on your negative qualities and attitudes this way. Make sure that your affirmations are always positive; leave the negative talk and vocabulary out completely. You may feel silly using them in the beginning, but science has proven that they are worth using to improve your performance and life.

A good positive affirmation is a constructive way of reprogramming your mind and turning perceived weaknesses into strengths. There are few things better in this world than leaping over the barriers that have imprisoned your mind. There is incredible power in daily affirmations. I would say use an affirmation for a month to let it properly sink in—three to five times a day is a good ratio—said in a mirror or during your quiet, introspective time.

I was far from perfect when I started, but thanks to daily affirmations, I grew into the person that I wanted to be. Your mind is capable; all you have to do is point it in the right direction and not be afraid of your personal power.

Creating Your Dynamic Vision Board

One of the best tools that I discovered to keep my mind on track was my vision board. Again, this was not something that anyone I knew would even consider. It may seem like a silly thing to do, but there are exceptional reasons for taking the chance and doing it anyway. A vision board is a simple tool for mind conditioning. It involves a piece of large paper that you transform into a collage of images of items that you want and goals or milestones that you would like to achieve.

Vision boards can be as simple or as complex as you want them to be. You can have one of them or several, depending on your goals. You can affix the "typical" images of super cars, mansions, and other material things you may want in life or perhaps images of family, love, and the vacation of your dreams. It is completely up to you. The goal is to create something personal and attainable and something that touches your soul.

Vision boards can be theme-based, they can be general, or they can detail exactly what you want out of life in the coming years. It all depends on you and what you want to create. My vision board has been instrumental in my goal achievement. By considering what is on my board and connecting with these goals emotionally, I have worked harder and longer on the right things, which has helped. There is a real sense of personal empowerment when you can stick anything to a board and then make it materialize.

I Had to Learn the Power of Vision Boards

A lot of people talked about vision boards, but I didn't understand what they were or what they meant. In 2012, I remember hearing someone talk about vision boards, and I did my own. I put a picture of a beautiful mansion on it. It was a beige color. It was over 6,000sf with tons of bedrooms and a huge backyard. It made my heart happy!

A few years ago, I was living in a nice 3-bedroom condo, but I felt it was time to live in a larger, more beautiful house. One evening God was speaking to me about changing my zip code. The average person would have rejected this notion if they were anywhere close to where I was at that time. My credit wasn't good due to my student loans and personal bankruptcy, and I didn't have a mortgage or even a preapproval. But God was telling me something else. I said, "Ok God, I'm going to go look at some places, but if I am going to look, I'm going to look BIG!" I'm found myself looking in the most affluent part of New Jersey. I scheduled an appointment with a real estate agent immediately the next morning.

When I arrived, I remember looking at the house, and all I could say was, "Oh my God, I want this house." However, there was this little thing inside of me (the devil) saying, "You're not going to get this house." And it kept coming, "You don't have a mortgage; this house costs 1.2 million dollars. Your credit is not where it needs to be." But I kept saying, "This is my house."

I remember coming back to the house the next day, walking around the outside and praying, asking God to bless me. I remember thinking about what I could do and how good I would feel living in the house. I thought about the schools my son's would be able to attend, meeting new people and lifelong friendships, and of course starting a family. My money was tied up in other businesses, so I could not buy the house outright. But I put in an offer—an offer of "blind faith!"

At the end of the week, the agent called and said I was approved! I'm like, approved? He said, "YES! Do not worry about getting a mortgage, the landlord will finance you directly!" I was in shock. That was a true blessing from God. I moved into the house in 7 days—yes 7, the number of completion!

When I moved in, I looked at my vision board. I didn't realize until that moment that the house looked exactly like the one that was on my vision board 5 years earlier. A beautiful mansion, beige color, over 6,000sf with tons of bedrooms and a huge backyard. I saw the vision, added it to my vision board, took action, prayed and it manifested—now it's your turn!

- **Sit down quietly** and reflect on what it is you want to achieve in your life in the next year. Do not be afraid to aim high but understand that aiming high means that you will need the right amount of time to achieve your goals.

- Flip through your magazines, and print color images from Google to find images that support your goals. **Cut out and/or print the images that speak to you** and inspire you.

- When you are done, **arrange your images on your board** without glue to see if they fit. The images should tell a story, or they should indicate where your ideal destination will be in the next few years.

- Once you have arranged your images and removed the ones that do not make sense, take some time, and stick them down. **Decorate your board** and add inspiring text to it.

- If you want to, you can place a personal photo of yourself on the board. Then **hang it in a prominent spot**—the best spot that you can find— where it will be visible every day.

Establishing Your Vision Journal Routine

Now, a vision board can be used in conjunction with a vision journal, or you can choose to do one or the other. A vision journal is a like a board only, obviously, in notebook form. You can paste your collages on different pages; organize them by year, by theme, or goal; and add as many learning experiences to them as you like.

The vision journal is a lot more interactive because it can be used during and after every goal. I use my journal in conjunction with my boards to elaborate on the things that I want to achieve in my life. Sometimes it helps to divide your life into sections—relationships, finance, business, health—so that each area has its own goals.

Decide what you are going to use your vision journal for and engage with it every day. To establish your vision journal routine, you will need to sort out the following:

- When will you look through your vision journal every day?

- How much time will you spend thinking about each goal or image?

- Will you add notes to your journal every day?

The morning is a great time to look through your vision journal because it acts as a motivation tool for the rest of the day, and it helps you plan. Most people fall short because they fail to plan. The planning stage is critical to acquiring the things that you want in your life. Most negative mindset people will not accept that this is possible, so they never even reach the point where a plan can be made.

A vision journal will help you uncover your deepest needs, wants, and desires. It will facilitate your transition into a proactive, positive mindset. Fill it with power thoughts, affirmations, goals, and images that inspire you towards your goals. These practices are associated with building a vision for your life. It is a method for planning that allows you to set directional goals for yourself so that you can reach an endpoint. Update your goals often and add to them as you grow as a person.

Holding Yourself Accountable for You

This is your life, and you only get one of them. You have to hold yourself accountable for your success. Since deciding that I wanted to be successful, I have held myself accountable for my actions, thoughts, and emotions. I have completely rejected the idea that poverty and failure will be a part of my life. It is HARD—unbelievably hard to take responsibility for yourself and hold yourself accountable, but it is necessary.

Accepting responsibility means knowing that you are not perfect and using tools like vision boards and journals to help you constantly grow. You can only achieve real freedom when you are completely in control of yourself. You are only in control when you are responsible.

Your inner world and your outer world need to be aligned. Responsibility is a gift from God and one that allows you to move in any conceivable direction. Treasure it!

- **Being self-aware is the first step to realizing your accountability.** YOU create what you experience, and you build your life. No one else does it for you.

- **When you are accountable, you realize that life is about action, NOT reaction.** Being a passive protagonist in the story of your life will always end in hardship.

- **Admit when the negative, painful experiences in your life were (at least in part) your fault.** You have to take responsibility.

- **Admit that you are afraid at times.** It is perfectly normal to be afraid. What is not normal is to allow that fear to dictate how our lives will turn out. You can choose to overcome fear and design the life that you want.

Though life is a wonderfully external experience, it all starts with what is inside you. If you fail to gain control of your inner life, you will always fail to control your outer one. That means accepting responsibility for who you are, where you are, and how you got there, right now.

I would never have had the courage to work toward earning millions if I had not accepted responsibility and designed my life. I knew what I wanted, so it made my choice easy. Either I could move forward and make things happen, or I could allow fear and doubt to destroy me and keep me from realizing my true potential. I chose self-responsibility! I chose to design the life that I wanted, build relationships and grow. Key #6 discusses this in detail.

KEY # 6

Designing Your Life & Strengthening Relationships

"If you don't make the time to work on creating the life you want, you're eventually going to be forced to spend a lot of time dealing with a life you don't want."

—*Kevin Ngo*

From Unplanned to Roadmapped

I have always found it insane that people shy away from planning. Imagine being put in charge of your friend's bachelorette party. You would spend ages planning to get it right. If you did not plan it properly, you would probably not even show up because you would be so embarrassed.

Now imagine how much more important your entire life is to you. If a plan is the ONLY way to get from point A to point B with your bachelorette party, surely a plan is what is needed for your life. All successful people plan their lives. They have long-term plans and short-term plans. They have itemized lists, vision boards, and vision journals. They have yearly, monthly, daily, and hourly plans. Every moment of their life is considered currency, and they know how to spend it in the right places.

When you really think about it, success is just that. It is the ability to set a goal (destination) and to move in that direction (time). Once you have outlined where you are going, you have to figure out how to get there. In essence, you have to run and treat your life like a lucrative business. This requires strategic planning and a lot of it. Success demands that you transition from "unplanned" to "roadmapped" right away.

If you have no goal, then you have no endpoint or destination. You do not know where you are going, how long it will take, or what is required to get there. Visually, it is you sitting in a car with a full tank of gas and no idea which direction to head in. If you have no plan, then you have no route to your destination. You may know where you want to end up, but you do not know how to get there, how long it will take, or what you will need along the way. It is you driving around with an empty tank of gas until your car comes to a halt in nowhere land.

You have to prepare for the life that you want. To do this, you need both of these preceding elements, or you will fail. **DESTINATION + DIRECTION x TIME APPROPRIATION = SUCCESS.** It is a simple equation, and yet people don't do it.

Life Strategy

Do you have a life strategy? I used to think that planning every moment of your life was insane, and then once I got ahead, I realized how INSANE it was to never plan your life. When you do not plan to have the kind of life that you want, do you know what you get? A life that you do not want! Failing to plan your life quite literally results in a 100% chance of leading a life that you do not want for yourself. That is a motivating statistic.

If you do not have a life strategy, ask yourself why! Who told you that it was okay to exist in this world in unplanned oblivion? Society? The same society that wants you to be an average, poverty-stricken worker bee. It makes sense then to do the opposite of what is normal for you and the people that you know. Individuals that plan their lives are massively successful!

Creating a personal life plan is a great way to give yourself clarity, balance, and a peace of mind. I cannot even begin to express how much less stressful it is to live in a goal-oriented world. You never waste a moment of your time feeling helpless or trapped. I believe that as we live and experience different things, a very clear image forms in our minds of where we would like to be one day. This is your ultimate life vision. Surely if you can make this life vision come true, you should be working at it right now.

The truth is that you can make almost any vision that you have for your life come true. Think of your life as a story—what do you want it to be about? A good life plan is extensive. It details each year and every milestone that you want to reach. It constantly changes according to your ability to grow as a person. I would encourage you to sit down and create your life strategy. Then you can set goals, determine outcomes, formulate priorities, and build action plans.

Begin with one sheet of paper and your name in the middle of it. Brainstorm the rest! Start by writing down everything you have experienced so far and the lessons that you have learned. Then use your life purpose, goal-setting skills, and the techniques you have learned in this book to outline a long-term strategy for yourself. Set goals at 20 years, 15 years, 10 years, 5 years, and 2 years. Bring it all back down to 1 year, and then fill in the gaps with pertinent details. You should have a very clear understanding of what you are doing now and what you will be doing next week, next month, and even next year.

Getting from A to B in a World Full of Zs

How do you succeed as a lion, when all around you there are passive zebras? This is the most challenging conundrum of all and something that I found to be a surprisingly difficult part of my journey. As I succeeded, I had to leave people, places, and experiences behind. It started slowly until eventually, I realized that my success was distancing me from certain friends and even family. Zebras will always gaze at you in confusion; they simply do not understand the calculated, strategic, action-oriented ways of a lion. They find safety with each other; you find safety knowing who you are and what you are capable of doing. Both are very different ways to exist in the world. So how do you get from A to B when you are surrounded by negative, passive people?

- **Align with other lions.** All lions need a pride because hunting together results in more meat for everyone concerned. In the same way, you need to align with other success-oriented individuals, because together you can create more money.

- **Distance yourself emotionally from the zebras.** Lions do not need advice from zebras because the chain of command works upward toward the lions, not downward toward the herd. It can be tempting to take advice from passive people, but that never turns out well. In this scenario, you have to take the lead because you know better.

- **Practice the habits of lions.** Other lions sit and watch; they know the coming and going of the zebra herds and are always in control. In the same way, you need to adopt the habits of successful people—planning, strategizing, vision boards, and journals. These are just some ways you can stay motivated and heading in the right direction.

It was a very big change for me to reject my passive existence and adopt a proactive approach to my life, but it worked! Fortune does favor the bold and brave because it takes courage and fortitude to plan every moment of your life.

Exercising and Implementing Lion Habits

I did not say it was going to be easy. If it was, no one would have to exist as a zebra. I have found that being a lion has pushed me to perform in my life in ways that I could never even have imagined as a zebra. Until you are there forging your path, you just do not know.

You must master the art of creating, exercising, and implementing lion-like habits. You have to go hard! I feel that I am the true definition of going hard. People say they are going hard, but they are not. What are you doing each day that is pushing you to your goal? Are you writing your goals down and following the plan? Are you exercising what it requires? Society does not teach us to "Go hard."

Society trains us to work slow and steady and not to get stressed. Society teaches us to work very hard for your boss. Society does not teach entrepreneurs how to really go hard!

For example, when I produce events, I go hard. Many people will say their event wasn't successful and that no one showed up. So, I ask them these questions. How many flyers did you hand out? How many people did you reach out to? How many times did you post and were they paid to post? They would say, "Oh I handed out about 50 or 100 flyers and no I didn't want to spend money on paid ads." Well, that's NOT going hard!

Lion habits would cause you to give out 10, 20, or 30,000 flyers and put out hundreds of social media posts—not a few, and not only free posts. Going hard will have you do it yourself if no one can do it for you or if you cannot afford to pay someone. Lions are not waiting for anyone. Lions don't wait and sit around at the mercy of others. Lions take action and invest in their success.

What Is the End Goal?

Lions start with the end and answer the question, "What has to happen for my event to be successful?" Then, they do that. Lions take risks and are determined to make it happen by any means necessary. You are going to fight for it! You will eat, sleep, and breathe whatever you are trying to do. You are going to push forward no matter what.

Moving from goal to goal, and from plan to plan, takes a ton of work and discipline. The rewards, however, are phenomenal. You cannot compare them at all to the rewards that you receive when you are a passive person who gets something right. Real rewards come from real dedication, planning, and action.

Practicing Acceptance and Freeing Yourself from Guilt

As a side note, but one that I find is extremely important in the grand scheme of things, is the issue of guilt. I do not know why people avoid this subject, but I am all about truth, and genuinely helping you is going to require some.

Guilt creates resentment, and it can manifest in a number of ways. I found that when I really started performing—and my life started rapidly changing—I became engulfed in this guilt, and I could not understand why.

- **Success is a personal triumph, but it leaves people behind.** The more you succeed, the harder it will become for the people around you. Understand that while you can help them, you are not responsible for their personal success.

- **Guilt is a self-inflicted emotion.** Do not doubt your hard work or success, because you feel like there are "more deserving" people out there. You have figured out your plan and have made it come true. You deserve every dollar you earn.

- **There are lots of different types of guilt**—social debt, unfulfilled responsibility, monetary debt, and experiencing rejection from friends because of your success.

I had to make a tough decision as I reached success to walk away from friends and family—period! People say it's lonely at the top, and I experienced that firsthand. What I realized was that my friends were great people, but they were great for hanging out and doing "regular" things. Fun for them was movies and the Chinese buffet. LOL! It was fun, and I do these things now, but I went through a season where I didn't want to do those things.

I knew I could never get to where I wanted to go by just doing "regular" things. I wasn't regular. I wanted more. I wanted a more luxurious life. I dreamed of being a businesswoman, but I just wasn't a dreamer—I was a doer! They were dancing through life and didn't dream. They were fine with living a "regular" life. If they were not fine, it's probably because they did not have these keys and did not know how to make the necessary changes.

People who don't dream or want more out of life may not realize it. This can be due to circumstances, or, not having learned to master certain skills. My social circle wanted to party; I wanted to plan. I wanted to work. I wanted to get out my pen and paper and write. I wanted to create and meet to plan the next move, and they wanted to hang out and have fun.

If I could go back and do it over again, I would probably do it a little differently. Maybe I would not have shut people out, but simply hung out and enjoyed social things when the time was right. Sometimes I feel like I missed out on young adulthood because I was so focused. Yes, I have felt regret and guilt along the way. I regretted missing out on some social things and relationships. I felt the guilt when people expressed that they were hurt by me not being around enough.

However, to become the person I was meant to be, and achieve what I am called to do, I had to let go of these feelings and forgive myself for both hard realities and the mistakes I made. I didn't handle every situation or conversation well. I realized that to keep moving forward I had to accept some of my mistakes and let go of guilt for not getting it right every time.

Stop Doubting Yourself and Accept That You Are Powerful

Then there is the kind of guilt that I ran into—headfirst. It is funny how you doubt yourself when you achieve something great. You can feel like it happened by accident, or it was due to someone else's influence. Accepting yourself as a powerful leader and a successful person can be one of the hardest things in the world.

You have to accept that YOU are the driving force behind your success and that you deserve every positive thing that happens to you in your life. No one should be able to take away your achievements, not friends, and not family! Accept that you are a lion and BE that person. Stop thinking of yourself as a poverty-stricken person who is struggling and trying to learn how to succeed! Either you are succeeding, or you are not. With the right plan, of course, you are!

If you fail to align your personal identity with other successful people, you will experience guilt. You will feel like an imposter, like a zebra dressed in a lion's skin. Reject that—you are a lion! Guilt only leads to resentment for the achievements that you will work so hard to secure. Do not allow yourself to distort this process and turn it into something negative. It is a red flag that I want you to look out for. Free yourself from "success guilt" so that absolutely nothing stands in your way, and every goal is another step towards your destiny.

Your Life Plan

A life plan offers you the opportunity to predictably outline every destination and every direction that you will move in during your life. That means that you can say with near-perfect certainty that your life will be successful.

You must become a strategic life planner. You must become obsessed with planning, scheduling, goal setting and achievement, and sharing this process with as many people as you can. I know that by now, you are already eager to get started. But there are still many important keys to learn. Success means learning and implementing all of the keys if you are going to reach ultimate success. Consider the elements that go into formulating an adequate life plan:

- What is that overarching purpose that flares up inside of you, bursting to be realized? This will guide all actions and decisions as you outline your life strategy.

- What is it that you want to achieve in your life? What is your ultimate vision or the end of your life story?

- Outline how you will achieve these things by working backward with reliable timelines. What do you need to learn? Who do you need to become?

- Then, based on your vision board and journal, put together a timeline for the next 20 years. The next 5 years should have their own vision boards and journals, along with clearly defined goals and action paths.

- Finally, you should have a 1-year plan that correctly outlines exactly what you need to do every single day to reach your ultimate goal.

The most important thing for continued progress is to have a non-negotiable habit of creating and executing a daily "to-do list" for every single goal. This process is simple to record and difficult to realize.

At this stage, I think you understand what it takes to attain success. And while it is true that many financially successful people do not plan to this extent on paper (they are naturally strategic), you will find that they lack success in other areas of their lives. I always have multiple projects going on simultaneously. One of my greatest secrets to success is that I can work on 10 projects at once if I have a plan for each one. Then, I purposely do something each day to keep all 10 things moving forward. I commit focused time to each one, and over time they get done.

For example, I have a national magazine called *Women Doing it Big* in Barnes and Noble, Books-A-Million, and on newsstands nationwide. This magazine is literally produced by me and one consultant. We do have a couple of writers, but what I'm producing quarterly takes some magazines 30, 40, or 50 people who take up an entire office floor to get what I get done with just one other person. This is because I have mastered the art of delegation. I have mastered the art of planning for each thing. Everything has a to-do list, and everything has a budget.

You Must Master "The Budget"

As you reach success, people will assume that you have money, money, money! That means when people come to you, and if you say that you don't have money, you will be frowned upon. People will say, "I thought you were a millionaire" as if you have an endless supply and a flow of money that is always available for whoever wants or needs it.

But true millionaires that are building wealth, understand that there is a budget for everything. Anything and everything I do has a budget. If someone asks me for anything and it's not in the budget, then there is NO money for it. You could have a million dollars in the bank, but if someone asks you for a loan, the answer is "NO," it's not in the budget. You have to have budgets for everything, and you only spend within that budget.

If something is not part of my master plan, the money will not get spent on it. It doesn't mean that I don't have money, but if it's not allocated towards a current project budget or overall master plan, it will not get spent. You have to master the art of saying "NO" if it's not in the plan.

So, if you are doing something, give it a budget. Say an item or event is budgeted for $1,500, you do not go outside of that budget unless you make money within that budget for ongoing things. That's the key to success. Do not go outside the budget. I don't care what happens. This discipline maximizes profits and minimizes or eliminates unnecessary spending and lending, which work together over time to build wealth.

Building a Winning Team

You often hear so much news when a big player gets traded in the NBA because when players change teams, it affects both the teams involved and the entire league. In the same way, a sports team is built, any major effort will take a team. I focus on building a team to ensure that I have the people I need around me. I am not just talking about people who work day-to-day, but consultants, graphic designers, an event team, hair and make-up team, production team, camera crew, and all these different people that are necessary for what I am doing. You have to have that team available at arms-reach to get things done to achieve your goals.

Building a winning team is never easy because no one is going to have the same love, drive, and energy as you. This means you will have to work with people who will only give you 80%. This means that you will have to hire and fire often. You will have to deal with difficult people who "switch" on you and trust me, I have had to deal with many.

However, even though dealing with people can be tough, you still need to work with people, so be smart. Protect yourself by switching passwords often. Never become too friendly with people who work for you and DO NOT share your personal business! Remember, you must maintain a fine line between employee and friendship.

Also, and this huge, when I am looking for someone to add to my team, especially an assistant, every person has a probationary period where I look for many things, but one supercritical thing. I look for people who will be just as happy as I am when my new book comes in the mail or a new shipment of products get delivered. I look to see if the person is genuinely excited for me when new opportunities for me arise. It shows me their motive. Are they here for me or here for themselves with an ulterior motive?

When hiring someone who will work close to me, especially support staff, I like hiring entrepreneurial mindsets. However, I make sure that they are not only there for their own gain. I always look for my own "Gail." That person who was what Gail King was to Oprah Winfrey in the beginning. Gail started as a player on the team ready to help in any capacity—even though she and Oprah were friends, but over time, she elevated in her entrepreneurial gifts and endeavors running businesses for and with Oprah. You want people who are strong but who understand that your brand and business is first when they work for you.

When you hire consultants, you have to make sure they are genuine and that they are down for you and won't sabotage you. You will have to go through a lot of people. You have to make quick decisions and let people go when things are not cool. Never let the frustrations of team building keep you from building a winning team. You need a team. You absolutely, positively cannot do it alone!

Achieving Social Advancement

There is nothing scarier than social advancement, but it is something I came to value after I realized just how much of an impact your friends and social circles have on your life. We all have dreams of taking our lives as they are now and making them better. Success is hard, and as I said, to reach the next level, you often must to leave people behind. Sometimes if you want to improve who you are, you have to improve who you know. That is just a universal truth that exists in this world. I am not saying, "Cut them out completely," but be mindful of them. The friend with a negative, self-defeating mindset can cause a lot of heartache for you—the person trying to stay focused and succeed.

Friends can affect your self-esteem, your potential, and your mindset—so do not think for one minute that they do not matter. I had to let go of a lot of friends that were not happy for me when I started breaking away from the poverty mindset and gaining wealth and success. I guess I cannot blame them for that, but it certainly puts things in perspective. Life is hard enough without having to justify or defend yourself against friends (and family) who do not understand what you are trying to achieve.

To achieve real social advancement will place you squarely in a new income bracket. Life is always about who you know and who knows you. When I hit the luxury market, the people I met really changed things for me. I began to see and understand that to continue in my field, I had to mix in new circles. It was the best thing I ever did. Once you change your circle, you change your situation. Not only was I more motivated to succeed, but I was suddenly surrounded by peers who understood my independence, drive, and entrepreneurial spirit. They motivated me instead of making me feel unhappy about the success I had secured for myself in my life.

Social advancement works in the same way as financial advancement. You should always be looking up and searching for new people that you can learn from and thrive alongside. I would not be where I am today if I did not develop the habit of making new friends in high places.

The Importance of Healthy Relationships

A large part of being a successful person involves your family, but I also know that families can be difficult. Family usually gives you advice, feed your emotions, and provide you with a social support base, but they are also the ones who can hurt you the most. However, when I use the term "family" in this chapter and throughout the rest of the book, I am not necessarily talking about a family that is your direct bloodline. I have learned that you can build close family-like relationships that are far better than your real family relationships.

Focusing on Family Dynamics

As a rule, you should consider yourself one of the most important members of your family because you are a leader. That means if your family is ever in trouble, you can help them when you can and within reason. As the leader, it's also okay to have moments of pain, moments you feel weak, and even moments of stress, but once the dust settles, you will have to pick yourself up and be strong for everyone. But DO NOT carry other peoples' stuff! Leaders must allow their family to fall, learn, and grow on their own and figure things out. This will help them. You cannot come to their rescue all the time.

Personal and Family Success

Family dynamics are rarely perfect, but in an ideal world, your family would be thrilled (at least most of them) that you are working towards success. The problem, of course, is that once success visits, everyone expects a piece of it. Success is not like a cake—you cannot just give it away. Sure, you can give or loan money to people (when it makes sense), but this cannot become a regular thing.

You can show someone how to do it, but you cannot put in the work for them. They have to act on their own and learn the keys to become successful.

- Only help those family members that support you and want to learn the keys to become successful.
- Only loan what you can afford not to get back.
- When you loan, make sure they know it is a loan and give them a date when it must be returned—no excuses! If they do not return the loan based on the agreed date, never loan them anything again!
- Keep the perpetually negative family members at a distance, or they will try to tear you down or tell you what to do with your life. Most of them will never see or understand your growth. They will see you as the same little boy or girl from back in the days.
- Communicate with and stay close to family who love you and who value your opinion.

Family relationships are an instrumental part of your life. The family does not go away when you become successful; if anything, some may draw closer. Make sure that your family does not "feed" off your success, as it will diminish your ability to grow. Make sure you are not just feeding your family circle but that your family circle also feeds you. We must intentionally build and simultaneously demand healthy family dynamics, where all give and receive from life-giving interactions.

When interactions are healthy, you serve your family in ways that will bring growth to everyone. Don't forget about you first, but do all you can to help your family on their personal journeys. Give them this book to read! If you all reach for success together, you grow together, build together, and "break bread together." These are basic relationship rules, and yet we don't follow all of them.

Relationship Advice for Power Women

Intimate relationships can be awesome, messy, passionate, chaotic, fulfilling and insane—sometimes, all at the same time! With that said, it is critical that you understand that your success is contingent on the person you CHOOSE to give your time to. If you are in a relationship with someone, understand how they can hurt you if they do not have the right mindset.

When it comes to relationships, there are simple priorities. First is your relationship with God. If that is not right, all of your other relationships will be off. Next is your spouse. No one can build you up or tear you down as much as your life partner. I learned a lot along the way and have had quite a few unhealthy relationships, but I learned a lot, and I am still learning. But the most important thing I learned is that you MUST CHOOSE WISELY! Do you have the same faith, beliefs, and values? Do you both want to achieve success? Do you have the same work ethic? Are you both willing to do what is required to live the life you deserve? If not, you will be in constant conflict and disagreement.

If you get into a relationship with someone who has never worked hard or who is stuck in the zebra herd with a trapped mindset, it can hurt you. It is ok to be a lion and grow with a zebra, but the zebra must be willing and open to change, or their mindset, habits, and limited vision may hurt you or slow you down. However, it is unrealistic and unfair to think or demand a person to completely change who they are immediately after they meet you. Yes, this can happen, but it is often unrealistic, and it takes time. If you find true love or if true love finds you, allow the relationship time to grow—as a unit!

Ladies, Strong Does Not Mean Overpowering or Demeaning

When you are a powerful woman, especially when you are in a relationship, married, or dating, you may have it in you to overpower the one you are with. Yes, you need to walk in power, but you can share in power, recognize your mate, and allow them to also lead. There are times when women can dominate their husband or dating partner in an unhealthy way that can belittle, drain him, or set up an overly confrontational relationship. Trust me, I have had to learn this the hard way.

As women, we tend to repeat the same mistakes our mother may have made, feel the need to be so strong and independent, or practice unhealthy relationship dynamics. Let me be real for a moment. There are a lot of women that desire marriage but can be so domineering that it pushes men away. A strong man will desire and seek a strong, beautiful woman, but there is a difference between a woman of grace and strength, and a domineering woman who may be beautiful, but at the same time very unattractive because of the way she carries herself and interacts with him. You can still be very feminine, vulnerable, and strong all at the same time, but it takes practice and a commitment to change with a deserving partner.

Respecting Individuality

The reality is that God created unique people with different gifts and wiring, and we must respect that. There is also truth in that many times opposites attract. Sometimes opposites attract because they complement each other. There is nothing wrong if one partner is a powerful entrepreneur, and the other is not interested or involved in those efforts, if they are in agreement and supportive of each other and who they are.

Bottom line, if you find true love, do not expect them to be you. I always thought I needed a powerful man and wanted to be a "power couple." A Jay-Z and Beyoncé, a Barack and Michelle Obama. It sounds and looks good in theory, but there is a lot that comes with that dynamic. Most successful people would rather have a regular everyday person because success brings drama. I am not saying you cannot become a power couple overtime but become powerful in love and enjoying each other. Love them for who they are and what they bring to the table.

Growth and Healing

Also, understand that EVERY person brings some level of dysfunctionality into a relationship. We all tend to repeat the dynamics we saw growing up because that is our "norm." If a person grew up without a mother or father in the house, they missed important things. If someone was abused or neglected, they took damage along the way. This means people must learn and heal along the way.

We must be patient with both ourselves and our partners. We must foster ongoing growth and healing individually and as a couple. When we have challenges, it is good to see a therapist to work out issues like anger or bitterness. Don't sweep it under the rug; deal with it for both your personal and relational health.

Relationships and People Are Complicated

In my current relationship, he and I are both bringing decades of "stuff" to the table. He is bringing his issues and baggage, and so am I. We both have experienced a lot of pain and loss. We both have had so much hurt, and I didn't realize it until now as we are going through the relationship on a path to marriage, that someone must yield. Sometimes it must be him, and sometimes it must be me. There has to be a balance of yielding. Yielding means stopping yourself from saying or doing something to hurt your partner because of a moment of high emotion. Both partners MUST practice this. This can be hard, especially when one may be processing or venting something they need to heal, but at the same time it may be triggering pain for their partner.

You don't have to just practice yielding, but you both have to practice eating "humble pie." This is hard, even for me being in a relationship with a powerful alpha—just like me! And he is a stubborn Taurus—just like me! Alpha type personalities often have huge egos and fear being hurt because it destroys their ego and pride. There is a saying that ego stands for "EASE GOD OUT" and a saying that fear stands for "FORGET EVERYTHING AND RUN." Many people let this type of "EGO" and "FEAR" ruin them and their relationships.

The Power of "I'm Sorry"

I've learned that in relationships, two of the most powerful words I can say are, "I'm sorry." They can also be two of the most difficult or even painful words to say. But they contain power to turn situations around in both our personal and business relationships. They are difficult to say because recognizing personal mistakes or failures requires humility which is the opposite of EGO. Then FEAR often comes from the fact that we don't want to actually deal with difficult situations, especially when we are at fault. Lastly, in most conflicts and situations, usually both sides are at least partially at fault, and there have been times when I said "I'm sorry" to own responsibility for my actions, but deep down really felt the other side was the chief offender. This type of humility and strategy often requires growth but allows you to deal with all types of people.

Dealing with Alphas

Powerful alphas (and most people for that matter) are afraid to be hurt and have so much pride that it will break them to the core if they feel less than who they believe they are. When two alphas disagree, it can get really nasty, you operate from the flesh, and don't function in the love that God would want. You start operating selfishly and without a care for the other person's feelings.

When I am upset, I say some of the most hurtful things, and my partner does also. I learned this from my dysfunctional family, and he learned this from his. This is a direct correlation between both of our unhealed pain. So, I learned (or should I say that I am learning), that you have to be humble and constantly ask God to help you. You also have to reach out to others to help both of you as a couple and individually to process pain, heal, communicate better, and move forward in a healthy way. One of my therapists told me that it is ok to have a disagreement with your partner and even argue at times, but when you argue, act like God is sitting in the room watching the argument play out. Is He pleased?

There Are No Perfect People

Many of us (including me) were taught to create a list of the perfect partner. This creates a picture in your mind of what a relationship is supposed to look like and how it is supposed to be, but our picture and list are often unrealistic. It's too perfect, and relationships are NOT perfect.

I love my (prayerfully) future husband, and I can honestly say that he does not meet everything on the list that I created years ago. My list outlined this "perfect" man. He had a certain amount of money in the bank and perfect credit. He had NO baggage, NO children, and NO issues. He was God-fearing, the ultimate prayer warrior—and let's not forget he smelled good, tall, chocolate and handsome! He was my Mr. Perfect!

HA! Here is the reality. My man, although he is certainly God-fearing, and is tall, chocolate, handsome, and smells good (lol), he is far from perfect—but so am I. How do I expect perfection, but I am not perfect? You can say you want someone with a certain amount of money but, how much do you have? You can say you want someone with a perfect credit score, but have you checked yours recently?

For me, it is important to connect with someone who loves God! It is also important to connect with someone you can grow with. Your partner WILL make mistakes. They will not come wrapped in a perfect bow that is your list. Remember, like mine, they (and you) are bringing years of "stuff" into the relationship, and it is up to you both to learn and grow together.

No list compares to someone who simply loves and adores you and is committed. No list compares to connection. You cannot buy or force connection. The laughter, the friendship, the joy that an "imperfect" person can bring to your life is very hard to find. Will you love them through it? Will they love you through? The joys, the ups, and the downs? You can meet the most powerful, richest handsome man or the most beautiful woman in the world, but none of that means anything if you don't have a true connection. If you can't laugh, bond and genuinely enjoy each other's company, you don't really have anything.

Bottom line, if a relationship is worth fighting for, you BOTH fight, and try to make it work. It is extremely important to be patient and allow time for a relationship to go through growing pains. This is especially difficult for me. I am an impatient person that likes to get things done—NOW! Whether it's my business or in a relationship, I just want to get to that finish line, but there is a process, and everyone is not going to move at the same speed or pace. I tend to run my relationship like a business. This is so wrong, wrong, wrong!

Different people are going to come to a relationship from different places, not thinking the way you think and not moving the way you move. This can be very frustrating. Sometimes in relationships, especially when you are a strong and powerful person, and you try to explain something to your strong and powerful partner or your partner who does not think or process as fast as you, they may not be able to receive it. This may make you feel as though your partner is not valuing you or your opinion. However, you have to allow your partner time to process your opinion, especially if it requires introspection and changes on their part.

While writing this book, I struggled with putting information on my current relationship out there, especially because we are not married yet, and people are often quick to judge. But more importantly, I want people to understand that life is real, and this is where I am at today. Many successful women are struggling with dating and finding or keeping a mate. Many other women are in difficult or failing relationships because they haven't yet learned this key. I feel a responsibility to share what I have learned (and learning) and took a risk to help others. Regardless of how this relationship goes, the principles remain the same.

Building a Relationship with Yourself

You have a relationship with yourself, and even though society does not acknowledge it much, it is this relationship that steers you down certain paths. If you are constantly at odds with yourself, you are more likely to give up on certain things. Or if you are constantly disappointed with the choices that you make, you can end up disliking who you are. The good news is that if you nurture a good relationship with yourself and proactively look after yourself, things will get better.

- **Take time to do new things** outside of your home that make you happy without your partner or children.

- **Make time for a massage** or anything you enjoy to recharge and regenerate lost energy.

- **Let yourself exist in the places you want to exist in.** If you love reading, then read! Understand that you need it, and schedule it in.

- **Engage in a lot of physical activity.** It can be easy to forget to focus on your physical needs. Work out at the gym, take classes, and blow off steam. It is a great way to release stress.

- **Listen to what your body is telling you.** Sometimes stress, emotion, or pain come from weird places. Learn to listen to your body so that you can act to correct whatever imbalance has formed.

- **Have technology-free time.** Schedule in some quiet, relaxing time free of phones, televisions, radios, and outside news sources. Just be.

- **Spend time in nature.** I am a big believer in the human connection between man and nature. Often you can come back from a camping trip or another outdoor activity and feel completely recharged. All you needed was to reconnect with the natural world.

Building a good relationship with yourself is going to take time. Care about your appearance, your health, and your emotional state. You will have a lot to deal with in the coming months, which means that you will need extra care and attention. There is nothing wrong with making sure that you get what you need to stay happy, healthy, and goal-oriented. Do not work yourself to exhaustion, and do not sacrifice your future because you do not look after your own needs.

THE FINAL KEY
KEY # 7

Creating Opportunities

"A pessimist sees the difficulty in every opportunity; an optimist sees the opportunity in every difficulty."

—Winston S. Churchill

The world is full of opportunity, but it is also full of distraction. Most people are enraptured by the distraction and never get a chance to discover the opportunities that cross their paths. Often, fear, hesitation, and the unknown keep distracted people firmly in the same place. For those that want to change their lives by altering their mindset, the first thing that comes into sharp focus is opportunity. You are surrounded by them all the time, but it takes a real lion to spot one that will pay off.

The Opportunity Mindset Explored

What if I told you that more millionaires are made during war, economic collapse, and recession than any other time in human history. Why do you think that is so? The theory goes that people become so desperate that they are forced to look for opportunities. More people take risks, and many of them pay off big time—resulting in millionaires. In addition to those that become millionaires, many more move out of poverty and up the socioeconomic ladder to the middle or upper-middle class. Bottom line is that even in the worst of times, opportunity exists for people with the right mindset.

Don't be that person that chooses not to see the opportunities all around them. One thing you can count on is that around the corner, there will be something interesting and lucrative waiting for you—whether it is an idea, a business, or an investment.

One of the final keys is learning to recognize opportunities when they appear. That means you need to develop the ability to spot opportunity and discern which ones have the highest potential for your implied goal. An opportunity can be defined as a set of circumstances that make it possible to DO something. This is interesting because people that do not see opportunity are also passive and refuse to DO anything.

Proactive people, on the other hand, that have the right mindset are always looking for better ways to get things done. And that is basically what opportunity is for you. You will have all your goals, strategies, and tools in place, and as you walk along your life path, you will come across opportunities to get things done quicker, cheaper, or better. That is why you must learn to be aware of your surroundings so that when opportunity knocks, you are there to answer the door. In fact, I have learned to not even wait for opportunity. Instead, I create opportunities for myself.

Creating Opportunities

One of my key success ingredients is that I do not wait for opportunities. I remember wanting to be on more magazine covers, so I created *Women Doing it Big* magazine and got it on newsstands nationwide, in Barnes and Noble and Books-a-Million. I remember I wanted to see my name as "A Tiana Von Johnson Film," so I did not wait for a documentary deal. I figured out how to produce it, and I did it.

I remember wanting to be on TV, so I got a crew together and shot a docuseries--*Powerhouse* and sold it to NBC Universal. I wanted to do a beauty line but did not want to wait for an endorsement deal, so I created my own beauty line. I found a manufacturer, produced it, and sold it across the world. I wanted to get a gaming deal, so I created my own board game and started to sell it on my own.

One thing about me is that I do not wait for anyone to hand me anything. I create opportunities, and this is super important for everyone to understand. You can create opportunities every day. Part of creating opportunity is purposely building your team and people you align yourself with.

Choosing Your Alliances Like A Pro

In business, strategic alliances make or break people. In law, for example, the partners are constantly looking for formidable lawyers who will one day become senior partners. These are the men and women that will keep the company going with their vision, talent, and skill.

In the same way, if you want to truly be successful in this world, you must concede that you cannot do it alone. No matter how intelligent you are, you will never have all the skills it takes to be the "perfect" person.

That is why in business, partners often balance each other out. By making strategic alliances with others, you gain the benefits of their talent and skill while adding yours to the mix. A chef and a manager make exceptional business partners because one can run the restaurant while the other runs the kitchen.

Strategic alliances take time, and decisions in this area should not be hastily made. In an ideal strategic alliance, both partners benefit from each other's skills and resources equally. When one partner benefits more than the other, it will nearly always result in a sticky end. Keep your expectations balanced, and make it clear why both of you are there.

A good partner understands your niche like you do. They are an action-oriented person that is willing to try new things, and they are focused on relentless improvement over time. It can take ages to sync two visions together, but when it happens, it can be brilliant.

In life, you need to learn to choose your strategic alliances like a pro. The right partner in business will be a major asset in your growth strategy and will get you to where you have to be a lot quicker than if you were alone.

- Network at conferences, seminars, workshops, or practically any networking event or place where the "right people" will be.

- When choosing your alliances, make sure that you have created a strict set of criteria. All partners or affiliates need to pass through these criteria and align with your vision if the alliance is going to work.

- Evaluate every single potential partner. From responsibilities to education, experience, team ability, and more. Your partner should be the missing piece that covers your weaknesses with strengths of their own.

- You must see the partner as an individual and not just a set of skills for your business. You will need to work alongside this person, so it is best if you get along and share a similar vision.

- Having a partner is fine but, testing them first is better. Set an exit plan if the partnership does not work out.

When I first started my real estate business, I aligned myself with someone who was the wrong partner. He was driven by greed and personal success. All of his actions were self-motivated. I, on the other hand, focused on building the company and the brand.

After months of disagreements and fighting, coupled with the fact that there was a personal relationship, the partnership soured immediately, and things got ugly. After a nasty fight and court battle, I was left in a position where I had to make a major decision. I could either a) remain in the messy partnership until it eventually failed or b) pay him off and walk away, leaving me with nothing but my company name.

At that moment, I felt like Tina Turner when she ended her relationship with Ike Turner, and all she was left with was her name. In the end, I chose to walk away with nothing and keep my name, and that was the real beginning of my entrepreneurial journey. I was left alone and trying to figure out how to get it all back—and then some!

Never Tolerating a Missed Opportunity

I will never forget learning a fundamental lesson about opportunities early in my career. Opportunities come in all sizes and forms—as potential business, as people, and as places. You never know when an opportunity is going to arrive on your doorstep. The trick is to be the kind of person that follows every opportunity to its logical conclusion. I missed out on one that would have made me a lot of money. In the end, what I learned is that I should not tolerate missing opportunities like that.

The fixed mindset person always has a guard up when it comes to opportunities. This often resulted from false dreams and hopes that many people sell. This clouds vision when it comes to real opportunity.

Part of what I do is create opportunities for entrepreneurs. I often bring groups of entrepreneurs together to present potentially life-changing training and opportunities. Within these groups, there is always a group of close-minded zebras in the room. Their minds often race to roadblock ideas—it's too much money, it's a scam, or they get stuck on asking the wrong questions and not seeing how it is going to work? Bottom line is that they come to the table with a negative or closed mindset. First, they will talk themselves out of it, and then they will talk the person next to them out of it. Others will be all in until they get back home to their broke friends and family who talk them out of it. This is laughable at times but also very sad!

I remember doing a conference and offering someone an incredible opportunity to work with me. I'm someone with over a decade of experience and an amazing track record of building successful businesses. I would be the only millionaire now part of her life! I offered her the opportunity, and she made the investment! My mind raced. I was so happy to work with her and had so many ideas to discuss with her during our first session.

Within 24 hours she called my office explaining that her husband said NO. He said that it cost too much money, and they could not afford to do anything right now. My team explained to her that this is the reason why she should be working with me. She declined, and we refunded her money.

I was 1,000% sure that her husband was a closed-minded zebra, grazing through life with his head down, and working a job he hated. Years later, I saw her again. She was in the same position she was in when I first met her. She never launched her business, didn't generate any more money, and her husband was now working a second job to make ends meet. She said they were both depressed and on the verge of divorce. Go figure! My heart was saddened to see such a gifted person living beneath her purpose. When I looked at her, I saw a lioness, but she chose to live like a zebra along with her husband, who were both about to get eaten up by lions.

These are the types of things that hurt relationships. You don't have to have the same type of career or be together in business, but you do want a person who supports your hustle and trust you—even if they are not an entrepreneur. So, if an opportunity comes, yes, you have to express a wise plan forward to your partner, but you should not miss opportunities due to their closed mindset or be dissuaded by friends or family who also have closed mindsets. You must be like an opportunity radar and treat every new experience like there is an opportunity waiting in the wings.

- When meeting someone new, always assume there is a reason.
- When going somewhere new, always look around and gather intelligence.
- When going to a self-development seminar, come prepared with money ready to invest in something that makes sense for what you need.
- When something terrible happens, look for the opportunity in it.
- When something incredible happens, find the opportunity inside it.
- When learning something new, see where the opportunity takes you.

Most people are either in tune with their surroundings or not. You are either focused on opportunity identification or not. The good news is that you can train yourself to be alert all the time. For me, it is a conscious daily practice, but I can see why the best businesspeople in the world are innately like this. When you never allow an opportunity to dance past you, you leverage everything life throws at you. Believe me, when you do this, you will NEVER be short of money. This is especially true when you take all of the keys into account.

When they all work together, they become a powerful force for your success. These days I have so many opportunities that I often turn them down. But it works both ways! As your success increases, so will your opportunity ratio. Eventually, you will have to carefully pick the opportunities that come your way. That is why knowing how to seek out, identify, and leverage opportunities is a fundamental business skill for any ambitious person. Opportunities are there in the strangest of places. All you need is the right perspective, a creative mind, and the will to turn ideas into reality.

Reaching for Each Dream

The model is very, very simple. Maintain the correct mindset, establish your destination, establish your direction (or process), and REACH! The only outcome is a successful one unless you quit during the exercise or are missing one of the crucial elements of the process. Your life will be full of dreams by now. So full, perhaps it is scary to think about all the things that you will have to do to get there. So, simplify it. Find one core opportunity and leverage it to your advantage.

At a crucial moment in my life, when things were really difficult, I was offered a partnership that would have sorted out my financial trouble but would have made me no better than an employee all over again. I had two opportunities here to take the money and run or reach for my dream and create the opportunity for myself. I chose to reach and create opportunity. Anything less, and I would have been missing one of the crucial elements in my success strategy. If you learn to think like this, your decisions will be tough, but they will come through for you in the end.

Transforming Your Life Through Empowerment

Let's be honest. Empowerment is more than just a feeling. It is a state of being. I personally feel this way! When you can transform your life through personal empowerment, you can take on the world—and that is exactly how you generate more empowerment. It acts as a domino effect. Every time you set a personal, meaningful goal and achieve it, you prove to yourself that you can do anything. The result is a greater sense of empowerment.

It is also why it is so crucial to maintain flow and momentum in life. The more success that you generate, the more success you will be offered. That is the way things work in this world, and while you may believe it makes things easier, it does not! Being insanely successful means being incredibly empowered, and though this is the person you want to become, you must realize that it takes huge levels of self-responsibility, drive, and practice to get there.

I want you to understand that when you hit your stride, this is when it matters most. Do not let empowerment go to your head. Do not allow empowerment to rob you of potential opportunities. No one in this world is better than anyone else. There are people with money and people without money, and opportunities come from both places. You can transform your life through empowerment if you never allow it to go to your head. Self-importance is not a great trait, and it will not serve you well in business. Being confident, friendly, and humble will do far more for your reputation.

You have a real opportunity right now as you learn and incorporate the keys into your life. Take your first step down this incredible road, sort out your life, and start building. Never stop learning and searching for new opportunities. There are always ways to level up. Just when you think that you have hit your peak, a taller peak will loom in the distance. How high you climb depends on your ability to stay focused, humble, and willingness to learn. You stop growing when you stop learning. Never forget that.

Conclusion

"Every great dream begins with a dreamer. Always remember, you have within you the strength, the patience, and the passion to reach for the stars to change the world."

—HARRIET TUBMAN

The **Million Dollar Mindset** is a way of thinking and a way of life. The vast majority of people will never become a millionaire because they neither think nor act like a millionaire. Before you ever become a millionaire, you must see yourself as one. Then you have to plan your life to become a millionaire. This is not about winning the lottery or somehow getting lucky. It is about planning, implementing, and working hard. Having the right mindset is not about having a certain amount of money in the bank, but about living a life where you have the freedom to be you. To have this type of mindset, you have to train your mind to think this way.

Imagine going to the gym and using the treadmill to warm up and do cardio, stretch to get loose, and then doing five different exercises to strengthen your muscles. These seven actions would train your body to be efficient, flexible, and strong. The more often and intensely you did this routine, the quicker your body would be transformed. The same holds true for the 7 keys. The harder you go, and the more frequent you implement, the faster you will transform your mindset. These keys are the roadmap out of the drudgery of life and can give you and your family a greater sense of vision and hope. Hope is a beautiful and devastating thing. I have seen hope lift people to heights they previously thought impossible, and I have seen families crushed by the false hope that they placed in a broken system.

Society is broken. Placing your hope in a system that does not work, and that is designed to keep people stagnant and, in the status quo, is going to end in despair. Instead, you need to do what I did. Place your hope and your time, effort, and expertise somewhere that matters—in the life that you deserve to live!

Being Who You Are in a Confused World

Since you started reading this book, you have experienced my disillusionment with our confused, broken world. I did not grow up in a home where entrepreneurship was mandatory and not an option. I was never really shown what it takes to survive in a room full of lions. Yet, here I am. I believe that society was never built for people like me or like you. While everyone wants success, it is not within everyone's grasp. There are lions, and there are zebras. The real tragedy is that our entire society, from the school system to the financial system, was created to support lazy, unmotivated, and unreliable people.

The system is excellent if your only goal in life is to be a zebra—someone that never really wants much, never earns a lot, and never goes anywhere. If that is your dream life—a life of utter financial, social, and emotional struggle, then this is the perfect world for you. Or maybe, you are a lion that has been caged and forced to integrate with the zebras. Is this you? If so, you must breakaway NOW! Every moment that you spend in a broken system (the zebra herd) is a moment of your life that is being stolen away.

My advice is to be who you are—not only who you are but WHAT you are. Take the essence of you and find a way to capitalize on it. The only thing that works when the world is confused is when the people on it are not. That is why the only people that succeed are the ones that move against the system, take action, and change their mindset.

There is a reason why so few people are able to overcome adversity and become wealthy. They are trained from birth to have an utterly incorrect mindset. But society has changed. It's not perfect, but many walls have been broken down. If I find a wall that's not right, I tear it down, I go through it and so should you.

You need to be who you are and the best possible version of that. Person by person, my hope is that we all wake up from this nightmare and realize that it is up to each of us to start the chain reaction in our lives and communities.

The Ability to Grow into Your Dreams

Success does not happen overnight. It starts in the mind of an individual and eventually becomes a powerful driving force that it is eventually called into being in material form. Everyone has dreams, and whether they are huge or small, you have the potential inside yourself to make them come true. The missing part of that fairy tale is that it will not be easy. You do not wake up one day and know everything. First, you have to plan and move forward. Then learn from all the mistakes that teach you those lessons. Then you change and adapt and go after it again. That is why having the "million dollar mindset" is right because it allows you to grow into your dreams instead of keeping them at a distance. You can create a path forward so that as everyday rolls by, you inch closer.

My only wish is that you try and fail dozens of times so that when you finally do become massively successful, you can deal with the sheer weight of that responsibility. It is hard to be successful. Success is not a reward; it is a byproduct of correct planning, execution, and management. Like any well-built home, if you skip a few steps and build a house on a terrible foundation, it will come crashing down. Or like many people's lives, it will sag, walls will crack, and though it exists, every day, you know it is inferior to what it could have been.

Success Can Be Hard

You have been given all the keys to creating the life you want, along with tips and tools to be a millionaire and be successful in all areas of life. People have all kinds of ideas about success and money, but let's be clear. There is a very clear correlation between money and success. There are many clichés that success is not about money, and I agree with much of the sentiment in the sense that someone can be rich and miserable or successful in business but have failures in their private life. That being said, I've met very few poor people who "feel" or consider themselves successful. The reality is that money meets needs and opens doors to different experiences; this is undeniable. But don't expect an easy path.

Success can be hard, but it is worth it! As I was trailblazing, I have been blackballed, talked about, shut out of things, backstabbed by staff, stabbed in the face by others, gotten terrible press, lied about on my good name, and many other painful experiences. As a person with real feelings, this hurt. People will tell you to have thick skin, but it takes time to develop a thick skin. You need to go through a lot of heartbreak and soul-searching. There were times when I wanted to go back to my 9-to-5 because at least people liked me.

On my way to a place of success, being smart and pretty, the very things that God blessed me with actually felt like a curse. It made no sense how my gifts and hard work seemed to work against me, especially in how people treated me. At first, I felt like I had to dumb myself down, then later felt like I needed to defend my good name. As I grew in success, the attacks also grew, but I had to learn how to push the criticism and attacks to the side and build up that thick skin—forget thick skin, I needed to develop a protective armor to keep my sanity and keep moving forward.

It's Worth It

After everything I have been through, I can look you in the eye and boldly declare that it is worth it! When you have the freedom to decide what you want to do each day, when you have time freedom and are able to travel, it is worth it.

When you can provide a better life for your children, it is worth it. When you are no longer locked into the system of everyday redundancy, it is worth it.

I love being able to give back and see the smiles on people's faces. Even if it's something as simple as taking my team to dinner. When I helped my father for his record conventions as a little girl, I remember that he always sent my brother and me to get food for everyone. I didn't understand why. He was big on two things—paying people and feeding people. To this day, I am not big on interns and volunteers, I want to pay you and feed you, and I always do both!

Life is not about shortcuts or skipped steps. It is about finding a purpose, having a destination, and heading towards that destination with all of your might—developing and growing as age and experience gather behind you.

The ability to grow into your dreams is what I hope this book has given you. Please do not close the book and settle back into your old life. This is an opportunity. Perhaps the very opportunity that will spark the change that will ignite your passion. And age does not matter. In fact, the older you are, the more urgent it should be. I would rather spend a lifetime fighting to be the best at what I do, than a moment lost and confused, wondering why a broken system has let me down.

Finding Your Place Among the Stars

Everyone has a story to tell. Everyone has a destination to reach. When you look up at the night sky, do the stars push for a position? No! Each of them has a place, and each shines in its own special way. I believe that you have learned the keys and are now equipped to find your place among the stars.

You have the mind of a millionaire; you just need to turn those golden thoughts into golden actions. You have been blessed with unique talents, skills, and traits that make your mind an asset like no other. It is time you took a mortgage out on your mind and reinvest it elsewhere!

So, my challenge to you is this—reject your old mindset. It did nothing for you anyway. Look around; do you want to end up like everyone else? Then stop trying to be like everyone else! Instead, be who you are. Find out who that is and how you can contribute to a better future for yourself, your family, and your community.

If each of us had to take this message to heart and excel, we could change the stats. Our communities do not have to exist in such debt and social turmoil anymore. When you adjust your mindset, you adjust your financial disposition. From there, things like family dynamics, social circles, and potential naturally improve. I am not promising to give you a better life. I want you to commit to building a better life for YOURSELF.

Let's Review the 7 Keys

Key # 1: Deserving Wealth - Being "wealthy" is not a state of having money. It is a process of learning how to create, invest, and manage money. It requires learning, and it certainly requires time. We must order our lives in ways that bring money from our own efforts. We must be disciplined and constantly invest our time and resources to gain the needed knowledge to manage our money. Educate yourself, take risks, hire a coach but don't blame or wait for others. Be proactive, constantly grow, and keep moving forward. This positions us to deserve wealth.

Key # 2: Think Like a Leader – Every day we choose who and what we are becoming. Leaders constantly strategize for success and then take action. Their minds are never fixed but always growing, always thinking. Leaders take risks and accomplish great things when they succeed and learn powerful lessons when they fail. Either way, leaders keep learning and keep pressing forward. Leaders always begin the race—and after them comes everyone else. If you step out of the zebra herd and don your lion claws, others will too.

Key # 3: Finding Your Passion and Purpose – Great leaders are driven by a passion that comes from within and is fueled over time. Passion is linked with our life purpose that drives people to be persistent in the face of any obstacle. It overcomes procrastination and passivity to help them live their life purpose. If you are going to change your mindset and evolve to become a more capable, personally empowered person, you have to outline what your passions are. These are the stepping stones that will help you discover who the "real" you actually is or could be.

Key # 4: Overcoming Challenges – Everyone faces challenges, but how we react to them will either elevate us to greatness or drive us down into mediocrity. A negative person views challenges with fear, apprehension, and suspicion, while a positive person sees challenges as another opportunity to attain greater levels of success. You need to become the kind of person who can overcome and break through any obstacle. With persistence and the right mindset, this is not only possible but a "must" if you are going to stay on your success path. You have to learn how to reset your mind so that it works like a bee that is constantly motivated to find pollen to create honey.

Key # 5: Your Personal Internal Power – Everyone is born with different skills, talents, and ways to become richer and more successful. The map to success for every individual is always inside you. You must train your mind to act for the benefit of your life. Using tools like daily affirmations, vision boards, and vision journals will help you uncover your deepest needs, wants, and desires. It will facilitate your transition into a proactive, positive mindset. These practices are associated with building a vision for your life. It is a method for planning that allows you to set directional goals for yourself so that you can reach an endpoint of success. A mind that is changed and trained to be more successful, more positive, and more practical will almost always find a way to excel.

Key # 6: Designing Your Life & Strengthening Relationships – People fail because they have no plan. To live a great life, you must have goals and a strategic plan to achieve them. There is no accidental success. No one will ever hand you a great life. The life you want to live results from designing it and taking action. Your success will also be determined by your relationships—family, friend and intimate relationships. Make sure you are not just feeding your circle but that your circle also feeds you. Intentionally build and simultaneously demand healthy relationship dynamics, where all give and receive. Most importantly, make sure that you build a relationship with yourself. Care about your appearance, your health, and your emotional state and implement things to improve them.

Key # 7: Creating Opportunities – The world is full of both opportunity and distraction and you choose your focus. Don't wait for opportunities, create them. Never tolerate missed opportunities but seize them. You must be constantly growing, creating, and always seeing things that others don't. When you see the world through lenses of opportunity, building wealth and experiencing great success is just a matter of time.

Final Note

Your mind is what drives your actions. Whether you know it or not, you are operating on a program that has been on standby for too long. It is time to assume manual control so that you can begin to see the world as it really is. Once you are there, you can shape it as you like. If everyone takes responsibility for the state of their lives, we can make positive change happen.

I believe that your ideal life is out there waiting for you. But it is not ready-made, packaged, and sitting somewhere. Your life has to be built from the ground up. Every decision that you make will affect the directions that you take in your life. Without destinations, you will always wander lost. Use this opportunity to streamline your mind, recreate your life, and prove to the world that when an individual accepts that they are personally responsible for their own lives, great things can happen. You will find that once the momentum kicks in, you will burst out of the gates like a racehorse and never look back.

I cannot promise you millions or the life that I have built for myself, but I can promise you that if you give yourself half a chance, you will succeed. You have learned the "7 keys to creating the life you want." Now you must focus on these keys each and every day. Each one will build your mind and help you think, live and become a millionaire.

There is nothing I can do beyond this book that will change your mindset. These are my words and thoughts on paper, trying to prompt you to act and shift your way of thinking for greater success. If you are going to find your place among the stars like I did, then today is the best day to start. Now take these keys and turn them into reality! You know how to do it. I have walked you through the process, so get to it!

Tiana Von Johnson

References

https://www.brainyquote.com/quotes/oprah_winfrey_402113

https://www.goodreads.com/quotes/194269-einstein-wrote-that-insanity-is-doing-the-same-thing-over

https://www.brainyquote.com/quotes/nelson_mandela_391070

https://bigthink.com/words-of-wisdom/words-of-inspiration-from-albert-camus

https://www.fearlessmotivation.com/2018/08/06/you-never-know-how-strong-you-are-until-being-strong-is-the-only-choice-you-have/

https://www.goodreads.com/quotes/958951-if-you-don-t-make-the-time-to-work-on-creating

https://www.brainyquote.com/quotes/winston_churchill_103739

https://www.goodreads.com/quotes/5935-every-great-dream-begins-with-a-dreamer-always-remember-you

NOTES

Made in the USA
Middletown, DE
11 March 2020